BRITISH BATTLEFIELDS

THE NORTH

British Battlefields

Philip Warner

BRITISH BATTLEFIELDS
The North

Where battles were fought
Why they were fought
How they were won and lost

OSPREY

Published in 1972 by
Osprey Publishing Ltd,
707 Oxford Road, Reading, Berkshire
© Copyright 1972 Philip Warner

SBN 85045 108 6

The maps in this book are based upon the
Ordnance Survey map with the sanction of
the Controller of H.M. Stationery Office,
Crown Copyright Reserved.

Printed in England by
The Berkshire Printing Co Ltd, Reading

CONTENTS

𝕾

THE MAPS
with grid references and directions

(between pages 64 and 65)

I STAMFORD BRIDGE

O.S. Map no. 97, grid reference 720 552. The battle site is eight miles east of York on the A.166. The course of the battle is easy to follow for the main features are unchanged, although the present bridge is 400 yards downstream from the original one.

II THE STANDARD
(Northallerton)

O.S. Map no. 91, grid reference 362 981. Take the A.167 from Northallerton and after three miles the battle monument will be seen on the right of the road. By turning right at the top of this road you can make a complete circuit of the battlefield. Scotspit Lane runs east-west across the southern end of the battlefield.

III BOROUGHBRIDGE

O.S. Map no. 91, grid reference 669 393. Boroughbridge is seventeen miles north-west of York on the A.1. The battlefield is easily visited, as is the neighbouring village of Aldborough, referred to in the text.

IV OTTERBURN

O.S. Map no. 77, grid reference 880 940. Otterburn is thirty-two miles from Newcastle on the A.696. The battlefield is marked by the Percy Cross.

V WAKEFIELD

O.S. Map no. 96, grid reference 551 321. The battle took place under the shadow of Sandal Castle, two miles south of Wakefield. Visitors should turn off the A.61 where the sign 'Castle Road' appears. The best view is from the castle-mound.

VI TOWTON

O.S. Map no. 97, grid reference 379 479. The A.162 to Tadcaster runs right through the centre of the battlefield, and the visitor will note Lord Dacre's monument. His tomb is in the Saxon churchyard just to the south. An easily-visited and most memorable battlefield.

VII HEDGELEY MOOR

O.S. Map no. 71, grid reference 049 198. Seven miles southeast of Wooler. Insufficient detail has been recorded to make it possible to reconstruct the exact sequence of this battle. Percy's Cross is at the south-eastern end and Percy's Leap at the northwest. Take the A.697 from Wooler. Local tradition places the battle site on the east side of this road.

VIII HEXHAM

O.S. Map no. 77, grid reference 952 610. Take the B.6306 from Hexham. The battlefield lies between Linnels and Newbiggin.

IX FLODDEN

O.S. Map no. 70, grid reference 890 370. Turn off the A.697 to Branxton. The monument is approximately in the centre of the battlefield.

X NEWARK

O.S. Map no. 113, grid reference 802 535. Finding Newark is no problem, but the visitor will find that the battle begins on the O.S. map no. 112 and finishes on no. 113.

XI WINCEBY

O.S. Map no. 114, grid reference 315 689. Difficult to find. Take the A.158 from Horncastle to Skegness and turn off on to the A.115 for Spilsby. The site is 1¼ miles along this road.

XII MARSTON MOOR

O.S. Map no. 97, grid reference 491 525. The battlefield is clearly marked by a monument and lies along Tockwith – Long Marston Road.

XIII PRESTON

O.S. Map no. 94, grid reference 551 321. Easily traced, even today.

XIV ROWTON HEATH

O.S. Map no. 109, grid reference 445 645. Rowton Heath is just south of Chester and the visitor will doubtless follow up to the walls.

Note on map references

All ordnance survey maps are overlaid with an arrangement of numbered lines called the grid system, which enables any point on a map to be easily and accurately identified.

A map reference is given in two sets of three figures, for example 396 112. The first two figures of each trio (39 and 11) are the vertical line (northings) and the horizontal line (eastings) respectively; they intersect in the south-west (bottom left) corner of the square to which they refer. Smaller divisions of the square are not marked but may be estimated, and the third figures of each trio (6 and 2) represent the 'tenths' of the lines east and north (right and upwards). Thus 396 112 indicates a point six-tenths east and two-tenths north of the intersection of northing 39 and easting 11.

As the side of a square represents one kilometre (1,000 metres) a tenth of that line must represent 100 metres: thus map references are correct to 100 metres.

INTRODUCTION

The battles described in this book occurred between 1066 and 1648, and took place in the area between Cheshire and Scotland.

Usually battlefields are a complete mystery to the visitor, for even if he knows when and where they were fought he rarely knows why, nor how they were lost or won. Still less does he appreciate how they may have hung in the balance or might have had a different result. The author of this book has vivid memories of the frustration of visiting battlefields in early youth without any clear guidance on the techniques of the period, nor the background causes which brought men to battle at that place at that time, nor the ultimate result.

The pattern of this book therefore is to fit each battle into the background of the time, to describe it and explain it; and then to bridge the period to the next northern battle. The battles which occurred elsewhere in the British Isles are mentioned and detailed descriptions of them are given in the other books in this series: the South; the Midlands; Scotland and the Border. Each book is self-contained and adheres to the main principle that a reader can grasp the sequence of events leading to a battle in his own area. Two of the most confusing periods in English history are the Wars of the Roses and the English Civil War. It is hoped that, by following the events and battles as described in this series, a reader will not only understand these eventful campaigns but also derive great enjoyment from visualizing those battles and considering what sort of a commander he himself would have made at the time.

The period covered in this volume is almost exactly six hundred years. Enormous changes took place in that time, not least the introduction of the longbow and, later, of gunpowder. The first battle in this book was a contest of immensely strong, adventurous men who wore little armour and hacked their way to victory with spear and battle-axe. Their weapons and strategy may seem crude and facile to modern eyes but the weapons, at least, required great strength, agility, and skill. The medieval warrior was an athlete of no mean ability.

Seventy years later the bow was coming into use, and contributed largely to the winning of the Battle of the Standard. Propaganda, too, played its part here.

At Boroughbridge in the early fourteenth century the longbow was then as established a weapon as the automatic rifle is today. Ground was surveyed and ranged to a yard; and the whole of a target area was blanketed with missiles.

Otterburn at the end of the same century was that most unpredictable of occasions, a night battle. All the usual mistakes were made.

Wakefield, in 1460, was almost a modern battle, certainly in a tactical sense. It had deception, surprise, and well-timed, concerted flank attacks.

Towton, the greatest and bloodiest battle ever fought on English soil, began with the longbow but soon became a vast personal combat, fought to a bitter end with no mercy shown by either side.

Hedgeley Moor and Hexham, although different battles, were so much part of the same campaign that they are treated together. Hexham had some interesting tactical aspects.

Flodden, although a medieval battle, in some ways resembled later, more modern battles. Readers will see some parallels with Marston Moor.

Winceby was essentially a cavalry engagement and was the forerunner of many a similar encounter. It was one of the smaller battles of the Civil War but had an importance which went far beyond the numbers involved.

Newark was a touch-and-go battle. It could easily have been a crushing defeat for Rupert but instead became a spectacular victory. By now guns and gunpowder were regular features of battles.

Marston Moor began in the evening in a thunderstorm and finished an hour or two later by moonlight. For most of the battle, the eventual winners thought they had lost and the losers thought they had won. With the dark, the rain, and the gunsmoke rolling over the battlefield, the confusion is not surprising.

Rowton Heath saw the end of the Royalist hopes in the first stage of the Civil War. Here again was a small battle, but its result was crucial.

Preston, which lasted for two days and part of a night, was the decisive engagement in the second stage of the Civil War. It was handled ineptly by the Royalists but brilliantly by Cromwell. Its redeeming feature was the courage and endurance shown in an otherwise not very creditable campaign.

The battles described, therefore, include most forms of possible tactical manoeuvre, and encompass a whole era of changes in weapons and armour. The English and Norsemen at Stamford Bridge wore boiled leather jerkins but little armour. Bows were few. Gradually the body became more protected, and shields became more cumbersome. A hundred years later the axe, once despised by the Normans, had become a cherished weapon, but for the next two hundred years infantry were considered vastly inferior in every way to cavalry. With the advent of the longbow in the thirteenth century infantry suddenly became extremely important and we find that, as archers, not only could they destroy cavalry at long range by pouring arrows on to them at about ten shots a minute, but they could also receive them with pikes and destroy them that way. But throughout the Middle Ages the knight, with his heavy complicated armour, and his magnificent expensive horse, was socially, if not militarily, supreme.

In the Civil War all the heavy armour was discarded, and horse and foot were scarcely hampered by the light body protection worn. Headgear, however, was still heavy. The Civil War produced excellent infantry, notably pikemen, but was essentially a cavalry war. Surprisingly, the Parliamentarians got the better of most of the cavalry battles.

A feature of medieval warfare not generally realized is the large number of foreign mercenaries who took part. But equally, there were numbers of English mercenaries serving in armies overseas.

The strategic geography of England played a very considerable part in the campaigns described in this book. Students of military history will be well aware of the importance of roads, ports, hills, and rivers. The fundamentals of strategic planning require roads for the movement of armies and their supplies: large numbers of men cannot move in cohesion over roadless country; they need ports for supplies and sometimes for tactical manoeuvres; they must avoid hills and marshes and therefore travel *via* the gaps, which thus become strategic points themselves; and they must be able to cross rivers by bridges and fords, use them for transport, and deny them to the enemy. Warfare, therefore, even in its crudest and bloodiest medieval form, was not haphazard but an elaborate form of chess with troops as the pieces upon a highly complicated board.

THE BATTLE OF STAMFORD BRIDGE

25 September 1066

The Battle of Stamford Bridge was as important as Hastings –
which took place less than three weeks later – but, because Harold
won the former and lost the latter, Stamford Bridge has been
relegated to the list of minor battles. But, if Harold had lost
Stamford Bridge, Hastings would not have been fought, and when
the Normans eventually came to grips with the Scandinavian
invaders a very different line-up of forces might have been seen;
William's invasion army would have been dispersed over the
countryside and he could well have been fighting at a considerable
numerical disadvantage.

Stamford Bridge is eight miles east of York, and there, in the
middle of the village, is a stone which commemorates one of the
bloodiest fights in English history. It is inscribed in English and
Norwegian:

> 'The Battle of Stamford Bridge was fought in this neighbourhood
> on 25 September 1066 – *Slaget ved Stamford Bruble utkjempet idisse
> trakter den 25 September* 1066'.

Even to-day, with a picturesque water-mill on one side of the river,
and a caravan camp on the other, it is not too difficult to visualize
that scene a thousand years ago. One can picture the long,
desperate, bloody conflict. Less easy to comprehend are the
extraordinary jealousies and motives that caused this battle and
made it so envenomed. Ironically, the losers had their revenge
when their conquerors were themselves beaten and destroyed at

Hastings so soon afterwards. But if ever there should be a haunted battlefield it would be this one.

For nearly four hundred years the inhabitants of these islands had suffered invasion and attacks from the north – mainly from what is now Scandinavia. In 787 the Anglo-Saxons – themselves once intensely warlike but now more settled – had suffered their first raid from the Vikings. This wild, adventurous, relentless Nordic people, who later became Danes and Norwegians, first terrorized by raids, then later invaded and settled in England. At times they were defeated – as by King Alfred in 870 – but eventually much of the North and Midlands was in their control. Gradually, however, they became absorbed into the English kingdom. Events were far from peaceful but, on the whole, the country was settled until, at the end of the tenth century, a fresh wave of Nordic invasions began, this time mainly by the Danes. Ultimately, a Danish king, Canute, ruled all England and Denmark and Norway as well, and, because he was supreme, gave his realm nineteen years of peace. After Canute's death it was a different story, and England was torn apart by the quarrels of his two jealous sons. When they both died within a short time of each other the new king was the ineffective Edward the Confessor, but the real ruler was Godwin, Earl of Wessex. When Godwin died, his son Harold, later to win Stamford Bridge and be killed at Hastings, took over Godwin's position and influence. This was 1054, and for the next twelve years Harold ruled England – though without a royal title – and ruled it extremely well. As a measure of Harold's fighting skills it should be remembered that he organized the conquest of Macbeth, the murder of Duncan, in Scotland, and also crushed a Welsh rebellion by chasing the rebels to the crest of Snowdon where they beheaded their leader, and brought his head to Harold's feet. He was said to be a small man, and modest; he was, in spite of his defeat at Hastings, a superb fighter and tactician.

But Harold had formidable problems. Some of them stemmed from his own lenience, for when he was defied by Aelfgar of Mercia, who twice brought the Midlands out in rebellion against

him, he forgave him and let him hold the powerful earldom of
Mercia, But another, more dangerous, problem arose from his
trusting nature. Harold's younger brother, Tostig, was Earl of
Northumbria, which then comprised most of the area north of the
Humber. Tostig ruled his earldom so badly and unjustly that the
people rose in rebellion, and in his place installed Morcar, the
younger brother of Aelfgar of Mercia, who, as we saw above, had
no love for Harold. When the rebellion was investigated, Harold
recommended (to the king, Edward the Confessor) that Tostig
should be banished and that Morcar should retain the earldom.
It was a remarkable decision, kindly and statesmanlike, but
disastrous folly for those times. By it Harold had made a bitter
enemy of his evil younger brother, and put into powerful league –
with over half the country at their disposal – two brothers who
were united in their hatred and jealousy of himself. Harold had,
of course, other troubles (from William of Normandy)*, but these
did not affect him at Stamford Bridge. The northern troubles
came to a head when Edward the Confessor died, and the Saxon
Council (the Witan) had to choose between appointing the late
king's ten-year-old great-nephew, or Harold, the man who had
effectively ruled the country for twelve years. They had no
hesitation over choosing Harold but immediately the appointment
was announced it set loose a storm of troubles. William of Normandy
felt that his own – admittedly dubious – claim should be admitted.
Morcar and Eadwine felt that they could now exploit the power
he had put into their hands, although he attempted to gain their
allegiance by marrying their sister, Ealdgyth. But the real threat
came from a totally unexpected quarter. Tostig, burning with rage
in his exile, had gone to Norway and persuaded Harald Hardrada
to espouse his cause.

Hardrada was a formidable figure by any standards. He was
generally considered to be the greatest Viking who had ever lived.
As the Vikings had produced generation after generation of fearless, skilful, immensely strong, and unwaveringly determined
fighters, this was praise indeed. 'Espousing Tostig's cause' meant

*See *British Battlefields: The South*.

that Hardrada was prepared to bring to England an invasion force that would defeat the English and install Tostig – and perhaps Hardrada himself – in Harold's place. And, as many countries already knew, when Hardrada set out on the path of war, terror preceded him, and victory with appalling slaughter was inevitable.

Tostig had been anything but idle in his exile, for already, with a fleet of sixty ships, he had been ravaging the English coast, beginning with the Isle of Wight, which he had sacked with impressive cruelty, and then moving up the coast to Yorkshire leaving a trail of slaughter and destruction. He had landed in the Humber but been driven back to his ships by Eadwine and Morcar. As soon as he was at sea, he had been intercepted by a fleet Harold had sent up after him, and in the ensuing battle lost nearly fifty of his sixty ships. The remnants of Tostig's fleet had then fled to Scotland where Malcolm, who owed his throne (after the death of Macbeth) to Harold, somewhat ungratefully gave Tostig refuge and allowed him to accept Scottish volunteers. Malcolm was probably glad to see some of his more turbulent subjects find themselves dangerous employment some distance away, instead of making life unbearable for their neighbours and their overlord, but it caused considerable bitterness between the two countries for many years.

The strength of Tostig's refitted fleet is not known but the general consensus of opinion is that Hardrada's numbered three hundred. This joined up with Tostig's force at the mouth of the Tyne, and together the combined fleet sailed for the Humber. Viking boats were renowned for their penetrative powers. When there was wind they crowded on every available inch of sail and drove before it – sometimes to spectacular disaster in storms – and when it was calm their crews rowed day and night on a shift system. The shallow draught of their ships enabled them to sail (or row) up narrow streams or creeks; they would be seen far inland one day and at a point along the coast 100 miles away the next. On 19 September most of Hardrada's vast fleet had sailed up the Humber, then slipped up the Ouse and disembarked at Ricall, some ten miles south of York. Swiftness and deception had enabled them to land unopposed, but Eadwine and Morcar were only too well aware of the threat, and had collected a substantial force at York. But it was in vain. When the two armies met at Fulford, two miles south of York, in a battle of which we have few details, the fighting was prolonged and bloody, but provided a devastating victory for the invaders. It was said that a hundred York clergy accompanied their army to the field to encourage them against the heathen invaders, and that they too fell in a general slaughter. But Hardrada did not sack York. For some unknown reason he merely demanded provisions and took hostages. He also left Norwegians to see that dead Vikings were buried with the correct warrior ritual. Possibly he thought that York would be his capital if he went on to take the English throne. The battle of Fulford had taken place on 19 September and the settlement of York on the 23rd. Now a further arrangement was made to exchange yet more hostages at Stamford Bridge. The choice of this venue seems to have been based on the fact that it was a nodal point – a cross-roads and a river-crossing combined. Even so, it seems a curious point to have chosen – well away from his base camp at Ricall and also from his new acquisition, York.

The invasion was well-timed. In Anglo-Saxon England the army was called up under the *fyrd* system which produced a rota of men-under-arms. At the end of the 'invasion season' – which was during the summer months – the *fyrd* was disbanded. Harold therefore had a difficult enough task in keeping the *fyrd* mobilized when he knew William was waiting with an invasion army in Normandy and the invasion did not come (it was delayed by contrary winds). Now a fresh threat developed in the north. At the best of times he would not have had enough men to meet the two threats simultaneously but now he was faced with a very difficult decision. Should he wait in the south for the greater threat from Normandy, which might arrive at any moment, but might, perhaps, be indefinitely delayed, or should he take a calculated risk and move up to the north where the invader was already on English soil? He decided on the latter. Hastily recalling as many as possible of his disbanded *fyrd* he rapidly organized his army. Then he set off north. On the way he heard of the disaster at Fulford and realized that there could now be no hope of a northern army to help him. He may well have suspected that his 3000 would be numerically smaller but he could scarcely have expected they would be outnumbered two to one by the northern host. He was himself, apparently, by no means physically well at the time.

On 24 September Harold reached Tadcaster. This small, attractive town on the Wharfe, famous for its brewery, has seen many armies, and the fugitives from many battles. Here Harold found his northern ships which had slipped out of the way of the Vikings. They would have been rapidly annihilated if they had tried to check Hardrada's fleet, but if the forthcoming battle went well for the English they might play a useful part when the Vikings tried to move away. Here, too, Harold was joined by other supporters. Morale, after the disaster of Fulford, would be at the lowest ebb, but the quiet, confident resolution of Harold – who always won – would be sufficient to send a surge of new hope through the fugitives. Harold wasted little time at Tadcaster. He had come to defeat the invaders, and the sooner he did it and went back to the south the better it would be for all. He marched straight to York, which, as we have seen, held only a token force of Vikings. It was a mere ten miles away, not much for an army which has already marched 200. He knew Hardrada had moved off eastwards, and doubtless suspected some cunning move to bypass him – and perhaps re-embark and land further south, possibly at London. But, to his astonishment he learnt that the Viking host was only a mere eight miles away, and apparently quite unsuspecting of his arrival. It was a golden opportunity – he would take them by surprise, for they clearly had no idea of his nearness. There would be a little murmuring from his men who had looked forward to a night or two in York, with its attendant pleasures, but there was no arguing with Harold's orders, nor any audible muttering either.

Surprise it was. Hardrada's army was scattered on both sides of the river, quite relaxed, and, as is the custom of an army in camp, quite unaccoutred for battle. Even the sight of the English vanguard did not at first cause alarm, for it was thought to be a contingent from York with news about the hostages. When the significance of the situation was grasped, Harold was less than a mile away. For a moment all was confusion, then it began to sort itself out. There was no time for proper deployment, and Tostig – with the bitter memory of two recent defeats – was not keen to invite a third; his suggestion was that they should fall back to Ricall. This, however, was not a policy to appeal to Hardrada. If Harold had never been defeated, he was not the only one; neither had Hardrada. The order was given to stand and fight.

The ground over which the battle was fought is easily discernible today, but the bridge which played a vital part in the conflict was not at the site of the present one, but was approximately 400 yards up-stream. The river was about forty feet wide in 1066, and was deep. The visitor will note that the east bank is slightly higher than the west, and will readily appreciate the river for the formidable obstacle that it was. Unfortunately for Hardrada, many of his soldiers were on the west bank, so even if he had wished to retreat down-stream on the far bank he would have had to fight a lengthy delaying action before that could be accomplished. The bridge was a wooden one, placed on stone pillars in the stream, and was apparently only wide enough to allow the passage of two men at a time. Hardrada decided to let the west-bank army take the edge off the English attack, then gradually fall back across the bridge to the east bank. The bridge would not be destroyed as it would be an ideal means of filtering the English army through to the slaughter. It was an excellent plan tactically, but it did not work out so well. The English attack was certainly blunted by the semicircle of Viking defenders. They stood like a solid wall, sometimes locking their shields like a barrier, at others, when the attack fell back, swinging their deadly axes in blows which went through arm, armour, and body. But the English were just as good, often better. This swinging of a razor-sharp, two-headed axe had more of the gymnast than the traditional soldier to it. The axe could be used as a boxer uses his fists, a short jab, a slippery parry, and an occasional full swing like a boxer's right cross. The strength, dexterity, and skill which was shown with ancient weapons, whether broadsword, axe, or pike, is difficult to comprehend today, but a hint of it may be gained from watching a modern woodman (who can cut and trim logs at a speed which makes a chain-saw seem slow, and who maintains an edge that you could almost shave with).

Hardrada's tactical plan went awry for two reasons. One was that his west-bank army were caught *in situ* without being aware at all that they were part of an intelligent withdrawal exercise. To them it must have seemed that they were merely the unfortunates caught on the far bank while their luckier comrades watched them fight it out. They were, of course, hopelessly outnumbered by Harold's army, who probably had a very fair idea that on the other bank the position would be the exact opposite. But fighting men fight, and that is it. They do not, however, fight any better for feeling that when their more important leaders decide the time is ripe they will slip back over the bridge and give the order for it to be demolished. Even if a man would die rather than retreat it is not encouraging to think that he has no choice in the matter. Doubtless the English were taunting the Vikings by telling them to get back while there was still time. And then, because there is a bend in the river at that point, the English broke through as the Vikings were manoeuvring to close a sudden gap. Suddenly the English were at the bridge and the half-circle of defenders was defending nothing of importance. Orders to retreat were shouted across the river. It is not, however, easy to retreat if you are under heavy and skilled attack; if you turn to look behind you to see where you might go that is when the spear comes through your guard, and you have no need for retreats. As the Vikings fell back they tried to cross the river with their weapons and armour, but the Derwent is deep here, and has steep banks. Many Vikings scrambled ashore but many were undoubtedly drowned in the way that always happened on these occasions – by others leaping down on top of them and treading them under, before perhaps suffering the same fate themselves.

But the bridge had not been destroyed. It is not, of course, easy to destroy a solid wooden bridge instantly, particularly a bridge which is built on stone pillars in the stream. Even unhampered, such a task can take a considerable time, and the Vikings, who were in easy missile range, were anything but unhampered. While attempts were made to destroy the bridge one man leapt forward to hold it. This latter-day Horatius was no ordinary man. Nowadays if you are a superb athlete you win titles, become a national boxing champion perhaps, or achieve worldwide fame in one sphere or another. Then, your only arena was battle, and, scornful of death, you showed your prowess. When your moment came you took it. And what better fate could a warrior wish for? As Macaulay put it, referring to Horatius who held the bridge over the Tiber against Lars Porsena:

> For how can a man die better
> Than facing fearful odds,
> For the ashes of his fathers,
> And the temple of his Gods?

But this Norwegian holder of the bridge was defending no city against the invader. He was a soldier who liked a fight and knew a good cause when he saw it. His name is unknown, and his feat is unrecorded in his own country – as might be expected in a lost battle fought far overseas. Doubtless there were others like him. But to the English, trying to cross that bridge, he was memorable enough. He did not trouble to stand in the middle or at the east end of it but, scornfully discounting all the advantages he might have had, stood at the entrance. Had the story come from his own side it would have been difficult to believe that one man could have held up an army, dodged all the missiles which were thrown at him, and remained unscathed. Had he held his position for a moment or two, then given way it would have been credible but he did more – he held it for a considerable time. One chronicler stated that he held it for nine hours; possibly he meant against nine men in succession. At all events he caused the battle to pause.

23

It is clear that there were no archers in the English army or his fate would have been swift.

But in the end it was subterfuge which destroyed him. An Englishman, realizing that this was going to decide the outcome of the battle, and perhaps the fate of the nation, obtained a boat in which he floated downstream. Doubtless the Vikings were unaware of what he was doing till it was too late. Once the boat-man was under the bridge he was able to stab a spear through the crevices in the logs. A lucky jab drove the spear into the Viking's leg and as the man staggered he was overwhelmed. It was said that the boat was a swill-tub and that for many hundreds of years afterwards there was a pie-feast each September at Stamford Bridge, in which the pies were made to look like old-fashioned swill-tubs.

As the English army poured across the bridge the Vikings made little attempt to restrain them. Instead they deployed for battle on the rising ground behind them, doubtless intending to drive their foes back into the river wholesale. But the mastery did not lie with the Vikings. Foot by foot they had to give way until the last phase took place on 'Battle Flats' – it still keeps the name – and it was a simple matter of skill, endurance, and determination. Perhaps, at this point the contrasting experience of the two armies told against the Vikings. Their mode of warfare was the fast-moving, intense terror-raid – at which they were superb. Now they were caught in a different mode of warfare – dogged, static, attrition fighting. It was not that they had no stomach for it – they had no experience or flair for it. But to the English it was meat and drink as would be seen on many another battlefield. At last the protagonists were almost face to face. Legend has it that Tostig was killed by Harold himself. At one stage in the battle – some say before it – Harold offered his brother a pardon and an earldom if he should lay down his arms. Tostig is reported as asking what Hardrada would receive and being told 'Seven foot of English earth, for he is taller than most men.' And that was what Hardrada did receive, for he was killed in the battle, possibly by a chance spear.

It was, by any standards, a bloody and heroic battle. The army which had needed over 300 ships to bring it in was able to leave in 24 – 500 men, perhaps, from 6000. Many of the Vikings were drowned in the last stages of the battle as they tried to leave a lost field, but the fate of the fugitives in that countryside can have been little less preferable, if at all. Harold burned most of their boats at Ricall but, once the fighting was over, was remarkably lenient to the defeated. Prince Olaf of Norway (the son of Hardrada) and the Earl of Orkney were both taken prisoner but both released and sent home. The dead were too numerous to be buried, and most were left to rot where they lay, but a few of the higher ranks were put in a tumulus nearby. Later, when the fields were cultivated, many of the other bones were collected up and interred.

It may seem curious that so much depended on a single wooden bridge. The explanation is soon obvious from a glance at the river. Not only are the banks steep but the bottom is muddy. A few optimistic warriors no doubt tried fording or swimming but their fate was soon a warning to others. The bridge was all important, but Hardrada – unused to that type of tactics – failed to appreciate the fact and lost the battle.

For the English it was a remarkable victory, won against over-whelming odds, for they were outnumbered, far from fresh, and attacking a difficult position. There was no opportunity for tactical skill, only for sheer bloody fighting. Probably they won through endurance and stamina. The Vikings had arrived by sea, where they had had all their exercise at the oars. Since landing they had had an easy battle and little marching. By contrast the English were as hard as nails, capable of marching 200 miles, then doing another eighteen in the space of about twelve hours. Stamford Bridge was, above all else, a lesson in the importance of battle-fitness.

THE BATTLE OF THE STANDARD (Northallerton)

22 August 1138

The Battle of the Standard, which took place just three miles north of Northallerton, Yorkshire, was one of the most extraordinary battles in English history. It occurred near the beginning of the most anarchic reign England has ever seen, for though the Wars of the Roses and the Civil War both tore the country apart, neither caused the widespread misery and dislocation of King Stephen's reign, aptly called 'the nineteen long winters when God and his saints slept'.

The battle at Northallerton was a contest of English against Scots but it was related to causes other than border warfare. In common with many battles and conflicts, the root causes were very simple and can be described briefly.

They originated when William the Conqueror brought over a host of self-seeking adventurers in 1066 and won the Battle of Hastings with their aid. He himself was strong enough to control his followers and wise enough to reward them with estates and tasks which would keep them out of mischief. His successor, William Rufus, achieved much the same stability by spectacular debaucheries during his short reign (1087–1100). The new occupant of the throne – a grasping opportunist – was Henry 1; and he was shrewd enough to keep his barons in order, although at that time, some fifty years after Hastings, they were sufficiently stable on their estates to be ambitious and greedy. And in an age when boredom was the greatest enemy, and warfare was the only form of recreation, outlet for ambition, and admired activity, it was inevitable that there would be immense turmoil if ever there was any relaxation in the strong grip of the monarch. That grip might be exercised by a combination of terror, blandishment, and bribery but it needed to be strong in all three of them. When Stephen came to the throne he was in the unfortunate – thus, weak – position of being an elected king. His claim was as good as Henry's daughter, Matilda – to whom he had been preferred in spite of Henry I's dying wish – but the fact that his right to the throne was arguable gave a semblance of justice to the manoeuvrings of every self-seeking baron in the land. The full horrors were not seen for some time, but later in the reign we have a gruesome chronicle of murder, torture, and general brutality. All this could have been checked had Stephen been firm, but he was generous to the point of idiocy, extravagant to the point of bankruptcy, and naïve beyond all recognized standards. His only saving grace was his outstanding personal courage.

Matilda, Henry I's daughter, whose claim to the throne had been set on one side in favour of Stephen's, had formidable allies. One was David, King of Scotland, the other was her half-brother, Robert, Earl of Gloucester. Both were undoubtedly honest, which is more than can be said for many of those who fought with them.

David crossed the Tweed and headed south in the summer of 1138. He had a large, wild army, and his ostensible reason for the expedition was to make Stephen restore to him the counties of Huntingdonshire and Northamptonshire which his family had forfeited in William the Conqueror's reign. The claim was somewhat tenuous but doubtless David thought he could honour a bond to see Matilda on the throne and also acquire handsome slices of territory for himself. The reaction of the north country to the arrival of thousands of marauding Scots was predictable; they had seen it all before and did not believe the invaders had any war aims except plunder. This cynical view was soon shown to be only too correct; the Scots ravaged Northumberland and north Yorkshire so savagely that it was obvious to all that this was yet another border raid on a massive scale, lasting longer, and better organized than most. If it were not checked, however, it could well become something more serious, that is a wild, undisciplined host of invaders who would eventually move south and create such a wave of destruction that the whole country would be set back several hundred years. Nothing so dangerous had ever been seen in England, not even with the Saxons and the Vikings; to estimate its effects one had to look to the invaders of the Dark Ages in Europe.

Fortunately for England there was a man available to check the onslaught, unsuited though he seemed for such a task. This was Thurstan, Archbishop of York. He was a man of advanced age, crippled, and ill at the time of the invasion. Nevertheless he would have taken part in the actual fighting if he had been able to force his deformed limbs into a suit of armour. Apart from his arch-bishopric he held the title of Lieutenant of the North, and, as the King's deputy by virtue of this appointment, he soon set about his task. With astonishing speed – possibly because bad news travels fast – he recruited an army from everyone in the immediate neighbourhood and from many further south who knew that their fate too was at stake. It is said that he enjoined his village priests to preach that this was a holy war; the appeal of a holy war is that if you fight in it you obtain remission for sins. Men fighting in holy wars tend to win or are defeated only at great cost. Many of the barons who rallied to Thurstan's side bore names renowned in warfare. They included Albemarle, Ferrers, de Lacy, de Mow-bray, de Courcy, and two names more famed in Scottish history than English, Bruce and Balliol. The rallying point was York and there Thurstan, a master of the whole art of war if ever there was one, provided a remarkable banner for them to carry into action. This was the redoubtable 'standard' which gave the battle its name. It was mounted on a four-wheeled wagon. At the top of the mast was a pyx containing a consecrated wafer, and from the two arms of the cross hung the banners of St Peter of York, St John of Beverley, St Wilfrid of Ripon, and St Cuthbert of Durham. A host of clergy accompanied the army.

Thurstan's cavalcade moved northwards from York like an avenging crusade. It halted at Thirsk, and Bruce and Balliol went out to parley with the Scottish king, and to offer him the earldom of Northumbria, which he had already claimed as his right. It is said that David, who knew that the north of England was in terror of his army, merely laughed scornfully. Bruce and Balliol were not impressed, and before they left to return to the English lines formally renounced their fealty to the Scottish king. When they arrived back with their bad news, Thurstan's army was neither surprised nor discomfited, but promptly set off towards Northallerton, marched through the township, and arrived at Cowton Moor three miles north; at the time the Scots were approaching the same area.

The battlefield is easily reached, for the A.167 runs through it, and there is a monument to the right of the road. It covers a considerable area, as would be necessary with the numbers involved, perhaps 15,000 Scots and supporters, possibly a thousand or so less English. Naturally enough, some of the details of so ancient a battle have been lost in the ensuing eight hundred years but it is not difficult to reconstruct the sequence from an examination of the battlefield. The Standard was placed on the hill to the north-east of the monument. As the battle is described as having taken place 'early in the morning', this would probably be soon after first light, perhaps between 5 and 6 a.m. Doubtless each side heard the other was on the move and both moved early to obtain an advantageous position in the coming conflict. In the event, there was little advantage to either side, but the Standard was placed at a conspicuous point, and was an encouragement to the English.

Both sides adopted the same formation; the front line were archers, who would discharge their arrows and then resort to other weapons; the second row consisted of spearmen; and the third rank was made up of knights and dismounted men-at-arms. In the first instance, David had wished to put armoured knights among the archers in his front line but his dispositions were wrecked by the men of Galloway who insisted on taking the foremost point in the battle, ahead of the Scottish centre. These Galwegians were a fearsome sight; they fought nearly naked, and their ferocity was proverbial. On the right of the Scottish line was a mixed force commanded by Prince Henry of Scotland, and on the left a contingent commanded by Earl Alan of Percy. King David, of course, took the centre.

The battle was crude in the extreme. There was no kind of strategy or tactics. As the two armies rushed at each other the English archers discharged point blank into the oncoming Galwegians. The effect of this was almost as severe as a volley of rifle fire. It seemed to be utterly unexpected by the Galwegians who had expected to come to close quarters and hack their way to victory.

The effect of this volley went far beyond what might have been expected. The Galwegians, checked by fearful slaughter in their ranks, but unable to come close enough to the archers to stop them, resorted to trying to fall back out of range. Unfortunately for their efforts, their leader, the Earl of Lothian, was killed in the hottest part of the fire and the leaderless division staggered and plunged backwards in hopeless confusion. Although unaccustomed to such intensity of close-quarter arrow fire, they knew that if they retired fifty yards or so they would be out of its range. But, as so often happened on other battlefields, as the front line staggered backwards it tangled itself with the second line and the two, hopelessly confused, presented a superb target to the advancing English. The result, in a short space of time, was that an enormous hole had been punched in the Scottish centre and only the third line, which had a stiffening of French and English knights in it – mercenaries, of course – stood firm. The Galwegians are said to have fled from the battlefield, but if so they must have got out to the flanks for they would certainly not have been able to break through their own rear lines.

But the Scots were by no means finished. Prince Henry, seeing the confusion in the centre, rallied the best of his army and charged down the slope on to the left wing of the English army. The ground he covered – the visitor will note – is low-lying and wet, and by the time the impetus of the charge was exhausted he and his men would be ripe for slaughter. There were, of course, well over

20,000 men on the battlefield and it must have been impossible to know at the time which way the tide was turning. Seeing the Scots advancing again, many of the waverers would come back in, some from the flanks, some from behind. The English centre, fresh from its initial victory would turn to its left flank and follow Prince Henry's charge. The Scots, blocked at the front, floundering on wet slippery ground – even in August – would then be attacked from flank and rear. This accounts for the slaughter which took place in Scotspit Lane, where bones and pieces of weapons were to be found many years afterwards. The Scots, now outnumbered, were hopelessly trapped between the two halves of the English army. The Scots were almost their own worst enemies, for where-ever there was fighting they plunged in, regardless of whether they were outnumbered or outmanoeuvred. So fierce was the fighting that King David and Prince Henry were able to slip away back to their horses and leave the lost battle. Only a few of their followers attempted to emulate them; the most part were content to carry on fighting in a lost battle for the sheer joy of combat. It is said that 10,000 men were killed that day, most of them Scots, but in addition fifty Scottish knights were taken prisoner. The only notable Englishman to be killed was de Lacy.

This battle has been regarded as somewhat of a mystery for centuries, and this is because the main grave-pits are behind the English position, although the English won. As we have seen, the explanation is simple enough. Scotspit Lane was probably a sunken road. As such, it may have been used as a defensive ditch by the English, or it may have been left for the Scots to fall into on their charge. Undoubtedly it played a bigger part in the battle than being a mere cemetery. Even today it has a slightly macabre look.

THE BATTLE OF
BOROUGHBRIDGE

16 March 1322

The years between the Battle of the Standard in 1138 and the Battle of Boroughbridge in 1322 saw many other conflicts at home and abroad, but at the beginning of the fourteenth century we find the same problems unsolved. Eight years before Borough-bridge the English army had been cut to pieces at Bannockburn, an event which would have seemed unthinkable in the previous reign (that of Edward I). There was no real threat to the throne from Scotland yet, but there was more than a hint that the anarchy which had not been seen for two hundred years in England might now be at the point of returning.

Over and over again in English history a pattern of events repeated itself. Whenever there was a strong king there was military conquest and firm government; but also a depleted treasury; and inevitably that strong king was followed by a weak one whose reign verged on anarchy. In the twelfth and thirteenth centuries strong King Richard I, who spent nine-tenths of his life fighting futile wars abroad but ruled over a stable country by sheer prestige, was followed by vacillating King John whose inconsistencies brought chaos. In the fourteenth century strong Edward I was followed by his weak son, Edward II, and later the country would see the might of Edward III dissipated by Richard II. The most dramatic events in this sequence occurred in the fifteenth century when the great conqueror Henry V left an infant son who grew up as Henry VI and was murdered in the Wars of the Roses.

Edward II, who reigned from 1307–1327, would have been a most unsuitable occupant for any throne. His father had exemplified all the military skills and virtues, his mother was a paragon among women. Edward II, however, was idle, obstinate, and feckless, sometimes cruel, homosexual; and attracted to friends who went out of their way to make enemies out of potential allies.

Boroughbridge was the result of one of the few occasions when the king showed any real purpose. His motive was purely revenge. His first and most irritating favourite had been Piers Gaveston, who had a trying habit of applying appropriate nicknames to leading nobles. The Earl of Lancaster was called, not inappropriately, 'the Actor', the Earl of Pembroke, 'Joseph the Jew', and the Earl of Warwick 'the Black Dog of Arden'. However, the three earls had the last laugh, for Warwick and Lancaster had Gaveston beheaded without any pretext but revenge. Edward II was compelled to pardon his friend's murderers for he had other and greater troubles on his hands at the time. All was in vain, however, for sheer incompetence caused him to lose the battle of Bannockburn although his army outnumbered the Scots two to one. But even the humiliation of Bannockburn did not cause him to forget his craving for revenge. To some extent it fostered it; it certainly aided him in achieving it. After Bannockburn Edward was virtually dethroned, and put under supervision. Lancaster, who had not even accompanied him to the battle, was put in charge of the administration. In his seven years of almost absolute power, Lancaster inevitably made many enemies. Nevertheless, it was not until 1320 that the lethargic Edward saw his opportunity. It occurred when Baron Baddlesmere refused Edward's wife, Queen Isabella, entrance to Leeds Castle in Kent. (The castle has no connection with Leeds in Yorkshire but both places derive their name from the Anglo-Saxon word for a stream.) Isabella, who later connived at Edward's murder and lived in open adultery with his supplanter, had appeared one night at the castle with an arrogant retinue and demanded entry. Admission was refused by the castellan, and the Queen gave orders to attack. The attack was repelled. (Centuries later a body was dug up near the entrance

to the castle. Although the feet were missing it still measured
6 ft 3 in.)

Edward stirred himself to action, raised an army and forced
the very strong castle to surrender in eight days. He was now full
of confidence. Realizing it was now or never if he was to regain
power, he set out to capture Lancaster and his friends. The barons
were not, however, prepared to be an easy prey and called up
their own supporters. Almost immediately there was a state of
civil war.

But the initiative, the power, and the luck lay with Edward. He
captured Hereford and Gloucester, which were centres of baronial
power, and called out a royal muster at Coventry. Lancaster,
however, knowing that he had everything to gain and nothing to
lose, assembled an army at Doncaster and set off south. He did not
get far. First he lost most of his baggage in a flooded stream (a
disconcerting event, as King John had found just over a hundred
years earlier), then he was by-passed at Burton-on-Trent, where
he held the bridge but overlooked the ford. Realizing that he was
outnumbered at this point as well as outflanked, Lancaster hurried
back north in search of reinforcements. His hasty move was
criticized, for it caused the prompt surrender of Kenilworth and
Tutbury castles and so alarmed one of his most valued supporters,
Robert de Holland, that he changed sides and joined the King's
army at Derby. Lancaster's position was weakening daily. His
confederates were undisciplined but self-opinionated. It is said that
one of them drew a knife on him in one of their 'councils of war'.
Lancaster himself wanted to make a stand at Pontefract, where
there was a strong though by no means impregnable castle, but his
supporters all urged him to fall back to Dunstanburgh, which he
owned, and where they might be joined by the Scots, who would
be very happy to embarrass the English monarch by supporting a
rebel faction. Reluctantly, and against his better judgment,
Lancaster agreed. His army crossed the Aire at Castleford, and the
Wharfe at Wetherby. It was then *en route* to cross the Ure at
Boroughbridge. Meanwhile, however, other events, fatal for
Lancaster, had been taking place.

35

Sir Andrew de Harcla, Warden of Carlisle and the Western Marches, remained loyal to Edward. On receipt of the royal writ he had called out an army and began to march south with it. He heard the news of Lancaster's northern march but at first merely planned to join the royal army and take orders. On 15 March however, when he had reached Ripon, he learned that Lancaster's army was now close by and was heading for Boroughbridge, six miles away. The Ure was said to be sixty yards wide at this time, and the road lay over a narrow wooden bridge, so the opportunity seemed too good to miss. There was a ford to the right of the bridge, which also needed to be blocked. Not the least of the effects of this move would be surprise, for Lancaster had no idea that Harcla was opposing him at all, let alone with such skill.

Although, like every town in Britain, Boroughbridge has altered with the years, it is still sufficiently unchanged for the visitor to visualize the battle clearly. Just under a mile east of Boroughbridge lies Aldborough, the old Roman town of Isurium, and this too had its influence on the battle, for the Romans had used the Milby ford to the east of Boroughbridge.

The extent of Lancaster's surprise may be gauged from the fact that his men were already finding billets in the town before they (and he) realized their onward path was blocked. The outlook for his army was ominous; not only was the way ahead full of enemy, and his force partially surrounded, but he knew only too well that Edward's other loyal supporters, the Earls of Kent and Surrey, were close on his rear. His immediate reaction was diplomatic rather than military. He sent a messenger to Harcla and met him for a lengthy discussion. In the past they had been good friends, and Harcla had benefited from the friendship. Strong inducements to change sides were offered to Harcla, but in vain. Harcla was no staunch loyalist – for a year later he made a fatal mistake which led to his somewhat barbarous execution – but at this moment he was not prepared to take the risk of joining an obviously losing side.

At the end of the conference, Lancaster cursed Harcla for a traitor and foretold that he would have an appropriate death. As Harcla was subsequently hanged, drawn and quartered, the prophecy proved correct but whether the prophecy was ascribed to Lancaster before or after the event is doubtful. With Lancaster's curses ringing in his ears, Harcla then returned to his own side of the river; hardly had he crossed than Lancaster's men tried to follow. But Harcla's archers were alert to this possibility, and though there was a brisk exchange of arrows it seemed that there was now a stalemate.

But Lancaster could not let such a position last. He needed to cross the Ure before Kent and Surrey closed on his army from behind. The initiative was taken by Humphrey de Bohun, Earl of Hereford. He led a charge across the bridge but was killed by a spear-thrust from underneath. The spearman was a Welshman who had doubtless never heard of Stamford Bridge nor his Saxon predecessor some three hundred years before. Next to fall was Clifford, and, somewhat disconcerted with two of its foremost leaders gone, the rebel army fell back from the bridge. Meanwhile Lancaster had turned to the ford where he hoped to force a passage. But here again the odds were against him. Harcla had anticipated the move and positioned his archers to cover every inch of the crossing. As the first party of Lancaster's men reached the river every arrow found a target. It was said that not a single horse managed to wet its feet in the river before it or its rider was hit by the deadly Welsh bowmen. Many of Lancaster's most valuable and influential supporters fell here, men like Lovell, Ellington, and Bernefield, whom he could ill afford to spare. But Lancaster was no coward, nor novice. Once again he threw his army at the ford, this time more widely dispersed and with a different timing. It made no difference. The bowmen had the whole area ranged to a yard; their bows might have been zeroed to their targets, so deadly and accurate were they. Lancaster's men began to waver, and some had clearly deserted: they had little wish to face that suicidal river crossing and then try to force their way up a bank protected by Cumbrian pikemen. But, by some unknown means, Lancaster was able to obtain a truce from Harcla and the following night it was Harcla who remained on the defensive while Lancaster's men slept peacefully, though perhaps apprehensively, in the town. During the night Harcla received further reinforcements from Yorkshire, brought in by the High Sheriff of that county, and the next day the two crossed the bridge and called on Lancaster to surrender. It was a bitter pill for a man who had ruled England like a king for nearly eight years, but there was no visible alternative; there was no fighting in which he could die spectacularly. He did not give in immediately for he thought he could find sanctuary in the chapel. Sanctuary was not, however, obtainable in every religious building, as Lancaster abruptly realized; and he was taken out and was soon on his way to Pontefract. 'The richest man in England' now dressed in an old gown was given a summary trial and, having been led to his execution on a 'lean white jade', was beheaded. Had he been less well-connected – for he was Edward II's cousin – he would probably have been drawn and quartered in public. Harcla did not survive him long; for he changed sides unwisely in the Scottish wars and met a traitor's fate. But whatever his morals, Harcla was a tactician of the highest class, as Lancaster saw only too well at Boroughbridge.

The battle was commemorated by a stone pillar which stood for many years in the main street of Boroughbridge. In 1852, for some unknown reason, the monument was removed to Aldborough, where it still stands. Visitors to the Boroughbridge battlefield should not miss the opportunity to look at the old Roman city of Aldborough.

THE BATTLE OF OTTERBURN

%

19 August 1388

In a long series of desperate border battles one of the most renowned was that of Otterburn. It was described extensively by Sir John Froissart, the French chronicler, who had spoken to many of those who had fought on each side; it was also the subject of heroic ballads. A number of these ballads were collected up in the mid-seventeenth century, and were published a hundred years later by Bishop Percy in 1765 as Percy's *Reliques of Ancient Poetry*. Two of them are 'The Ancient Ballad of Chevy-Chase' and 'The Battle of Otterbourne'. Both describe aspects of the same battle. Sir Philip Sidney, who lived between 1554 and 1586, knew them well and wrote 'I never heard the old song of Percy and Douglas that I found not my heart moved more than with a trumpet; and yet is it sung by some blind Crouder, with no rougher voice than rude style; which being so evil aparalled in the dust and cobwebs of that uncivil age, what would it work trimmed in the gorgeous eloquence of Pindar.'

Froissart's account of the battle, together with the two ballads from Percy's *Reliques* are given in full on pp. 119–57.

For this encounter to be celebrated in verse and song several hundred years later it must have been an outstanding piece of bloody warfare even for those days and for that area. It is not perhaps generally realized that when the border Scots and English were not fighting each other they were usually fighting equally fiercely among themselves. The picture of a peaceful countryside stirred to arms by an invader was less true than quarrelsome families having temporarily to forget their enmities and unite against a foe who might exterminate them all. The dirk – known very appropriately as 'the widow-maker' – would merely be turned towards a different target till the greater danger was past; the English, of course, were no less fierce and turbulent than their foes across the border.

However, Otterburn was also part of a wider conflict, which may be outlined briefly. We described how, at Boroughbridge, Edward's supporters were victorious and restored him to power. This state of affairs did not last long, and through apathy and stupidity he soon fell victim to the treachery and ruthlessness of the other side. Eventually he was murdered in Berkeley Castle. His son, Edward III, was of a very different character, and proved as great a warrior as his grandfather, Edward I. Edward III won the great battles of Crécy and Poitiers, but fell into premature senile decay. His son, the Black Prince, had predeceased him, so the next king was Richard II, a boy of ten. He, too, would be murdered after reigning twenty-two years, and the details of this crime, which took place at Pontefract Castle, would be a better kept secret than Edward II's death at Berkeley. But in 1388, when Otterburn was fought, Richard was far away and having his first brush with his rebellious subjects. The news of the internal troubles of England had reached Scotland and it seemed an ideal time for a border foray, if not for a full-scale war. The Scots, of course, would have been extremely unwise if they had not seized every opportunity to improve their military position against the English, and were always delighted to do so.

The Scottish army was mustered at Jedburgh on 5 August 1388. In order for the war plans to be kept entirely secret, the leaders resorted to a nearby church to confer. However, the English were not unaware of the preparations going on on the other side of the border and sent along a squire to obtain what information he could. The squire, who had disguised himself suitably, entered the church with the Scottish chieftains, and heard all their plans, but, when he returned to where he had tethered his horse, found it had been stolen. Naturally enough, he did not wish to draw attention to

himself by making vociferous enquiries so instead he set off for
England as he was. However, the spectacle of a man in boots and
spurs setting off to invade England on his own was a little too
obvious, and in a short time he had been overhauled, brought
back, and questioned. In the persuasive way which medieval
interrogators had, they encouraged him to confide in them the
English plans. The English, he told them, had only a small army,
and did not therefore wish for a straight confrontation. Instead,
they planned to let the Scots move first, then by-pass them, and
wreak havoc in Scotland behind. This policy would doubtless
bring the Scots headlong back, and give the English time to collect
a larger army against further trouble. It was, however, vital to the
plan to know the Scottish invasion route; if they came through
Cumberland the English planned to invade by Berwick, but if the
Scots chose the eastern route the English would head up through
the western side.

Greatly pleased by this information about the English strategic
planning, the Scots resolved to thwart it by splitting their army in
two and invading on both sides simultaneously. One half therefore
set off for Carlisle, led by the Earl of Fife; the other, which consisted of 3000 men-at-arms and 2000 infantry, set off towards
Durham. This eastern army was led by the young Earl of Douglas.
Both Scottish armies were very well equipped and armed, having
just received a large consignment of arms from France. Young
Douglas's army pushed rapidly through Northumberland, scarcely
pausing to destroy, but, when they reached the outskirts of
Durham, it was a different story. There the Scots slaughtered,
burned, and pillaged, and then returned towards Scotland with
their spoils. The raid had succeeded brilliantly. The English,
thinking this was the vanguard of the entire Scottish army, had
planned to check them at some point in south Durham or north
Yorkshire, and were taken by surprise by the tactics pursued by
the Scots.

So far the Scots had all the initiative, and, on the way back,
although burdened with loot and spoils, decided to take Newcastle.
Newcastle was lightly held, although its commander, Sir Henry

Percy, had hastily put it into a state of defence. The Percy family of Alnwick Castle were old rivals of the Douglases, and any encounter between the two countries was almost certain to bring these two antagonists face to face. This happened at Newcastle where the Scots failed to take the town but where Douglas succeeded in capturing Percy's pennon. The pennon was a long triangular flag carried on a lance; it served as a rallying-point for a knight's followers. If he was promoted on the field of battle, the point would be cut off, making it a banner, and he would become a 'banneret'.* The loss of a pennon was a serious matter, as Douglas well knew, and in a spirit of chivalry which was more often talked about than seen, he decided to give Percy a chance to regain it. He did not therefore hurry back to Scotland but instead paused at Otterburn and attacked the castle. His attempt was futile, for Otterburn Castle required proper siege equipment; but even then Douglas did not move on. Instead, he cut down trees and made a camp.

The site of Douglas's camp was just to the north-west of Holt wood, on a hill containing some ancient earthworks.

Douglas's delay may have had more to it than chivalry. Possibly his great burden of plunder was impossible to move quickly; perhaps he decided that if Percy wished to catch him up he could lose more than a pennon. Probably, too, he was reluctant to leave England without having one more good wholehearted fight.

Percy seems to have behaved with unexpected wisdom and caution. Perhaps he thought he was being drawn into an ambush; perhaps, however, he was merely waiting to assemble an adequate number of troops. He was apparently surprised to find the Scots had made so little progress.

By now the armies on this side were evenly matched numerically, though the Scots had the advantage in equipment.

Percy, once he had decided the time was right, hesitated no more. He arrived at the Scottish camp towards evening on the 19th. It was well-concealed in the woods and he did not realize

---

*There was no connection with baronet, which was a rank invented several hundred years later.

how close he was to it till the alarm was given. According to Froissart, Percy did not reach the camp till after sunset and first saw it by moonlight; this is unlikely, as medieval armies, like campers, usually liked to settle down for the night while there was still light enough to see what they were doing, unless there was some good reason to do otherwise. Percy, however, took an unusual step in that he decided on a night attack. Night attacks can be devastating to the opposition when they are accompanied by surprise, but they can be disastrous to the attacker who may fall into unseen natural traps, and also do as much damage in the dark to his own side as to the opposition.

Percy, perhaps because he was not entirely confident that Douglas might not receive reinforcements if the battle was delayed, decided on the somewhat ambitious plan of a two-pronged attack. One wing went round to the rear of Douglas's camp, led by the Umfravilles, the other, led by himself, attacked from the front. Unfortunately, the camp Percy attacked was not the main one at all but a baggage pound. Its occupants were soon slaughtered but in the time this took Douglas had led a large detachment round to the English right, skilfully avoiding the Umfravilles who had circled too far to the north. Just when it seemed that the English were winning, Douglas hurled himself on to their flank. The fighting now became bitterer than ever, but the English, although now hard pressed, fought with relentless courage. The sudden appearance of armed men, gleaming in the moonlight as they emerged from the trees, must have been an awesome sight, but a ghostly look is no proof against a sword-cut. Owing to the Umfravilles' error, the English were probably outnumbered in the main fight but soon the Umfraville party corrected its bearings and came to the Scottish camp. It was, by now, empty, so they left a guard – all of whom were slaughtered by the Scots later – and tried to find the others in the darkness and general confusion. Again, however, they took a wrong direction and instead of coming on to the rear of the Scots he arrived on the right of the now much-battered English. The only time there was a pause in this bizarre conflict was when the moon was clouded over. But, in the brighter intervals, the

English numbers were now beginning to tell. Douglas, however, at this point showed what a leader can do. Swinging his battle-axe he carved a path into the English army. He fell from four wounds but the inspiration was enough to set the Scots surging forward and the English reeling back. Sir Henry Percy and his brother, Sir Ralph, were both wounded and taken prisoner. The fighting still went on, but in small groups only.

The battle continued for most of the night and the next day the victorious Scots were hunting the English for prisoners worth a ransom. It was said that the poorest were allowed to go free which, if true, would make this unique in medieval battles.

Percy had attacked too soon, for the next day the Bishop of Durham came up with several thousand reinforcements. However, with their leaders captured, the heart had gone out of the English army and after a few manoeuvres the Bishop retired, leaving the Scots unmolested.

Various explanations are given for the English defeat, and all are credible. One was that after a march of thirty-two miles they had not the strength for a prolonged night battle; another is that they could not use their longbows in the dark; yet another is that the Scots had better armour and equipment for hand-to-hand work. But the most probable reason was that in an indescribably tough battle the better-trained army won. The Scots had been in the field for most of August, constantly fighting and on the move; the English in contrast were partly hastily-summoned levies. Froissart said of it: 'Of all the battles and encounterings that I have made mention of heretofore in all this history, great or small, this battle that I treat of now was one of the sorest and best foughten without cowardice or faint hearts.'

Otterburn, as Percy's army knew, is thirty-two miles from Newcastle (on the A.696). The 'Percy Cross', a monolith, marks the battlefield. Perhaps it should more appropriately have been called the Douglas stone for he must have been killed close by.

THE BATTLE OF WAKEFIELD

31 December 1460

The Battle of Wakefield was an unexpected, but extremely important, victory of the Lancastrians over the Yorkists in the Wars of the Roses. The term 'Wars of the Roses' refers to the series of increasingly bloodthirsty battles which took place between 1455 and 1485. Even after 1485 there were attempts to keep the conflict open.* Many historians consider that the Wars of the Roses were really over by 1471, for after that year there was an interval of fourteen years till the next major battle. However, the contest was not resolved in 1471; but for the time being no one was strong enough to challenge the holder of the throne.

During the first part of the wars, battle succeeded battle with steady frequency, and when one side was victorious the other knew its turn would come before long. The explanation of these extra-ordinary vicissitudes lies in the background to the conflict. Although with surprising consistency a strong king had been succeeded by a weaker one – often the former monarch's own son – the situation had never been as disastrous as when the warrior king, Henry v, died on a campaign in 1422 and the next heir was less than a year old. Worse was to come, for when the new king, Henry vi, came of age he was already showing signs of the insanity which was later to dominate his life. He was undoubtedly murdered at the end of his chaotic reign but the secret of how and when it happened was well kept. But it was not the folly and insanity alone

---

*As described in 'The Battle of Stoke Field' in *British Battlefields: The South*.

of Henry VI which caused the disaster of the Wars of the Roses; it was also the underlying weakness of his claim to the throne. This stemmed from the deposition and murder of Richard II by his cousin, who became Henry IV. Richard was a fool, and also arrogant, but can scarcely be said to have deserved his mysterious fate in Pontefract Castle. However, when his cousin took the throne there was bound to be a challenge to the line sooner or later. It did not come in Henry IV's reign, although he had other troubles to contend with, and it was smothered during Henry V's reign, for he was a brilliant and successful warrior king; it was even delayed in the reign of Henry VI for over thirty years, but when it came it tore England apart, and exterminated the leaders of many powerful families.

As well as the disruptive effect of weak sons following strong fathers, there was the even more disturbing factor of the weak sons choosing unsuitable friends. People are prepared to put up with a monarch's weaknesses but they are not so ready to accept the activities – and insults – of his cronies. As Henry VI's favourites had apparently contributed to the loss of France, it would have been wise for him to have chosen differently when their incompetence was brought home to him. But Henry, like many a weak man, was also obstinate. In 1453 he was loyally adhering to the Duke of Somerset although a wiser man would have replaced that unpopular but successful figure. In 1453, however, the king went mad. It seemed almost too good to be true – and it was. Henry VI's cousin, the Duke of York, who might be said to have had a better right to the throne than Henry, was promptly elected Protector of the Realm, the unpopular Somerset was put in prison, and it seemed as if all would be well, as York would soon succeed to the throne. Unfortunately for these hopeful thoughts, two things upset the prognostication. One was that Henry's wife, Queen Margaret, produced a son after nine years of barren marriage; the other was that Henry recovered his sanity after eighteen months' madness. Now, the position was worse than ever. Prompted by Margaret, who had an almost psychopathic hatred for the well-meaning York, Henry dismissed the Protector from office, and in his place put Somerset, who had been incarcerated in the Tower of London during York's period of power.

York was slow to anger but this was too much. He conferred with his friends and marched towards London. At the first Battle of St Albans he was completely victorious, and Somerset was killed. This, however, was not the end of the matter but only the beginning. Margaret was determined to remove York and his line from the scene so as to ensure that there could be no obstacle to her own son's taking the throne when Henry VI died. Battle then succeeded battle, but on 10 July 1460 the Yorkists won a crushing victory at Northampton which seemed to put the issue beyond doubt. Many people now felt that the country should be stabilized by York taking the throne. It was said, in support of this policy, that Margaret's son had been fathered by someone other than Henry VI, and that York would have to succeed sooner or later.

This was all very tidy and neat but it reckoned without Margaret who, after Northampton, had fled to the north where she knew she had friends. They included notable fighting names already mentioned elsewhere on other pages – the Percys, the Nevilles, the Cliffords, Dacre, and lesser fry. The army she assembled was said to number 10,000 (some gave it nearly twice that number), and it should be borne in mind that these northern soldiers had spent most of their lives fighting in one war or another. The problem was not how to make them fight and win, but how to control them when they were not so engaged. Their great asset seems to have been dash and mobility, and, though their opponents were by no means sluggish, it was Margaret's ability to exploit these qualities which brought her victory on several occasions. Margaret had an interesting combination of characteristics: she was French, she was a young woman, she had an astute tactical brain, and she was relentlessly and ruthlessly determined. Although not a very attractive character, she earns our admiration for her physical stamina, and unstoppable determination. When Margaret was finally beaten, eleven years later, it was because she had played every card in her hand but lost every trick.

But Wakefield was the hour of her triumph. Six months before, she had been fleeing for her life; now she had an army, perhaps 2000 stronger than York's. York had, in fact, badly miscalculated. He should have gone on after the victory of Northampton and led the armies himself to the north. There a few minor battles would probably have finished the Lancastrians for good. Instead he dallied in London, trying to legalize his position in Parliament. When he decided he must move he made the mistake of under-rating his opponents. His eldest son was occupied in North Wales, where Welsh Lancastrian sympathizers were becoming active, but would have been better employed with the main force. York appears to have been very careless – or perhaps preoccupied – for a large contingent of Lancastrian supporters from the West Country marched right across the West Midlands to join Queen Margaret's army at Pontefract. Margaret was quietly optimistic about the result but after her unfortunate and dangerous experiences following the Lancastrian defeat at Northampton she decided to stay in Scotland until results were announced.

York set out north on 9 December. On 16 December his vanguard brushed with the West Country army at Worksop. York's men were apparently taken by surprise, for many of his troops were killed. However, even if York had known the West Country-men were marching to Pontefract he could hardly have expected to meet them in Worksop. His own destination was Sandal Castle, two miles south of Wakefield. This once powerful castle is now an earth mound, but excavations are now bringing to light some of the stonework which has been obscured for centuries; it is an impressive sight. Sandal Castle was destroyed by the Roundheads in 1643, after surrendering, and its former glories are not easily visualized. But in 1460 it was immensely strong and when York reached it he may have been glad of the fact; when he sent probes towards the Lancastrian camp they had the worst of it in an encounter with the Lancastrians and were pursued right up to and into Sandal Castle. York therefore decided to take no immediate action but to sit tight and wait for reinforcements.

But the Lancastrians had sized up the situation well, and also knew the character of the men they were opposing. Sandal Castle was not provisioned to victual an army some 8000 strong and the Lancastrians had ensured there would not be much gain in foraging in the countryside. However, they had not the siege artillery to break a way into the castle, and if they waited to starve it out, even if only for a few days, half their unpredictable army might wander off elsewhere. Then, when York's son, Edward, brought up reinforcements from the Welsh border it might be the Lancastrian turn to be well outnumbered. They may not have known how short of provisions York really was but they probably hazarded a useful guess.

The battle took place on the open space between the castle and the River Calder which slopes fairly gently. This was then known as Wakefield Green.

The surrounding ground was heavily wooded, and this fact enabled the Lancastrians to practise a very simple deception. They split their army into two halves and set one marching towards the castle as if prepared to make an all-out assault. The other was concealed in the surrounding woods, where it took up positions unobtrusively.

The arrival of a much smaller Lancastrian army than he had expected was a welcome sight to York, and without delay he decided to demolish this threat to his comfort and stomach. The Lancastrians seemed to show no great appetite for a fight, relying on defensive work by the archers, and giving way as the Yorkists approached. York's army was, of course, being drawn further and further from the castle. Then at last the Lancastrians stood. As the two armies became locked in combat the rest of the Lancastrian army suddenly appeared from the flanks and rear, and hurled themselves on to York's surprised and outnumbered army. The timing was apparently perfect, and the battle was over in half an hour.

Tactically, this was a most unusual battle for medieval times. Its techniques were almost modern. They included subterfuge in luring the Yorkists out of the castle into an ambush, surprise and perfect timing in the flank attacks, and concentration of force at the right place and the right time.

York was killed, but whether in the battle or after it is not known. The story which evoked the most horror was the death of the young Earl of Rutland, who was killed in cold blood by Clifford. Apparently Rutland knelt and begged for mercy but Clifford replied, 'Your father killed mine so now I shall kill you'; and did so. Equally chilling is Margaret's treatment of York. His corpse was beheaded and his head displayed at the gate of York wearing a paper crown; it was flanked by those of the old Earl of Salisbury and the young Earl of Rutland. Wakefield was a bitter and revengeful battle and then and afterwards many old scores were settled by both sides. The pity of the Battle of Wakefield was that the best man of the Wars of the Roses was outwitted and killed halfway through the conflict. That was the Duke of York, who was the most stable, restrained, and statesmanlike figure of the period.

THE BATTLE OF
TOWTON

❧

29 March 1461

The Battle of Towton was the bloodiest and most bizarre battle
ever fought on English soil. Contemporary accounts gave the
casualties as 28,000. This may well have been accurate for killed
and wounded, and it is worth while bearing in mind that in a
battle of this nature only the lightly wounded would be likely to
recover. The number killed on the battlefield itself was probably
not less than 10,000, which is a staggering enough figure, for in
those times – with the exception of a man caught by a cannon
ball – killing was a laborious process. Most of the combatants
were protected by some form of armour, and mortal wounds were
not easily inflicted.

One of the bizarre features of Towton was that it was fought from
dawn to dusk in a snowstorm. It took place on Palm Sunday, 29
March, on a bleak upland and in a sodden valley; on this occasion
men did not merely fight men; they fought the elements as well.

Visitors to Towton and the neighbouring village of Saxton
today need little imagination to visualize the scene. Everyone of
note was there on that battlefield, and brought to it the feelings
of hatred, ambition, and revenge which had been stored up for
the previous five years. Many battles have been fought without
great feeling on either side; the armies of two separate interests
clashed and there was a battle. Men were killed and wounded,
issues were settled, and misery followed for many. But these
ordinary battles were lukewarm compared with Towton. Towton
was a bloodbath of hatred.

Up till the Battle of Wakefield in the previous December, there had been some semblance of chivalry in the Wars of the Roses. Prisoners had been spared, executions had been restrained, and there was an attempt to limit the slaughter to the leading figures. But after Wakefield the atmosphere changed. It had always been a precarious balance with so many mercenaries and so many veterans of the French wars, all of whom were well versed in the cruellest and most ruthless side of war. After Wakefield their behaviour differed very little from that of less experienced troops. Subsequently the casualties after Mortimer's Cross had been very high indeed, and after the second Battle of St Albans Queen Margaret made her seven-year-old son decide what form of death – axe, sword, or rope – should be inflicted on prisoners. Margaret had recruited large numbers from the wilder border areas and once the fighting began there was no possibility of restraining them, and precious little before or after.

It was, of course, extraordinary that, after the great and surprising Lancastrian victory at Wakefield, followed by another equally devastating win at St Albans, the Lancastrians should retreat to Yorkshire and be defeated crushingly within six weeks. Many explanations are offered but only one seems convincing. It was said that after the second Battle of St Albans (17 February 1461) Henry VI persuaded Margaret not to let her wild army advance on London. He may well have suggested it, but it seems unlikely that Margaret would have paid much heed to his reason, which was to spare the capital from the ravages of the Lancastrian army. There may, however, be some basis for the theory that she was afraid that she would lose her army in the capital, particularly if entry was opposed. A more probable reason was that, while she was regaining control after her victory at St Albans and collecting up her warriors, who were ravaging and plundering the countryside, she heard of Edward's surprising victory at Mortimer's Cross and decided that London was not the place nor the time right to fight his army. Margaret, it will be remembered, was never very confident about the Midlands and the South. She felt safer in the North, where she had previously won victories, and where she had a clear retreat to safety. Possibly her feelings were shared by some of her army commanders. The Elizabethan historian, Holinshed, certainly held that view.

As Margaret gathered up her forces and retreated to the north, Edward consolidated his position in London. He was staying near St Paul's, at Baynard's Castle* which had once been as important as the Tower of London. On 4 March Edward took possession of the crown and sceptre at Westminster. He was still only nineteen, but in experience and physical maturity clearly much older.

The Lancastrian error in not pushing on to London was now to be fully exploited. On 5 March Edward launched a recruiting drive; two days later Warwick was able to set off north with a powerful vanguard. Recruits poured in, partly because of hatred for the excesses committed by Lancastrian troops, partly because Edward's army looked like a winning side. In those days of limited economic opportunity or advancement men gambled heavily on being on the winning side in a battle. Then the victors would be rewarded by property taken from the conquered, and would hope to keep it. This made another round almost inevitable sooner or later, for the survivors of the vanquished would engage in almost any desperate enterprise to regain the little they once had owned, and perhaps to increase it. When therefore the order 'No Quarter' went around, as it sometimes did – and certainly did at Towton – it was welcomed as it was always assumed that the opposition would be the ones to be slaughtered and lose their goods. Edward arrived at Pontefract just before 25 March, and camped at Bubwith Heath. There he paused and organized his army which had been greatly augmented by recruits, and numbered at least 25,000; some sources gave a suspiciously exact figure of 40,660.† The Lancastrians were now at York but had no desire to be besieged there. The fashion of the day was to confront

---

*It was named after Baynard, one of William the Conqueror's entourage; at the moment of writing it is being excavated prior to being lost for ever in a 'development' plan.

†At the same time the Lancastrians were quoted as numbering 60,000.

the enemy in the open field or on ground of your own choosing. This, of course, is when your own superior handling of troops would tell, when you could outmanoeuvre your enemy, break up his formation, and demolish his forces piecemeal. If you are going to do this it will be as well if you have made the right calculations and have made every gain possible before the battle. A man who chooses to give battle at a certain place and time needs to be very sure of his estimates and troops, otherwise he may well find he is commanding a beaten army which should have avoided battle altogether on that occasion.

The Lancastrians had the advantage of choosing the ground and selected Towton Heath, two miles south of Tadcaster, twelve miles from York, It is easily found; the A.162 skirts one side of it and the B.1217 runs through it. Lord Dacre's monument on the side of the latter road serves as a battlefield monument. To the left, as you face north, is the River Cock, which will be noted as a fast-flowing stream between steep banks. The banks are deceptive and anyone trying to cross would be suddenly precipitated into much deeper water than he had anticipated. This would play a significant part in the battle.

Without knowing exactly where the Lancastrians were going to stand, but knowing it could not be far off, Edward sent a small force up to Ferrybridge, two and a half miles north-east of Pontefract to hold the ford over the Aire. Twenty-four hours later this force was surprised by a Lancastrian raid commanded by Lord Clifford. The Lancastrians killed both the commanders and most of the garrison. Clifford, who led the raid, was nicknamed 'The Butcher' on account of his cold-blooded killing of Rutland at Wakefield. The news of this reverse came as an unpleasant shock to the Yorkists and many began to regret joining the army. However, two dramatic incidents served to check this sag in morale and restore confidence. Warwick killed his horse and said that henceforth he would fight as a foot soldier; this removed the unpleasant suspicion that if the Lancastrians looked like winning the Yorkist leaders would be the first to leave the field. Then Edward announced that if anyone wished to leave the army he could do so now, though not later. It is said that no one accepted the offer, and doubtless everyone was subsequently glad of the fact.

Nevertheless, even with high morale, matters did not go well for the Yorkists. An attempt to retake the ford was flung back with heavy casualties. However, Edward was not to be deterred and sent a detachment to cross up stream, which it did at Castleford. Once Clifford learnt the Yorkists were across the Aire and his retreat to the main body of the Lancastrians could be cut off he fell back rapidly. Unfortunately for him, he did not fall back fast enough and, as he reached Dintingdale, was caught in an ambush the resourceful Fauconberg had quickly prepared for him. Clifford was caught by a chance arrow and killed, and the ambush closed in on his force. Only two or three escaped. The ruthlessness of Towton was already foreshadowed. Clifford's body was never discovered; possibly it was hacked to pieces by vengeful Yorkists, for not only was he credited with the murder of Rutland but was said also to have decapitated the dead body of York. Soon the remainder of the Yorkist army was passing through Dintingdale (which is eight miles north of the Aire). It was then late afternoon on 28 March. They marched forward whilst it was still light and took up battle formation at Saxton. On the other side of the valley were the Lancastrians who had what seemed a very good position with the left flank on the ridge close to the Tadcaster–Ferrybridge road, and the right flank on the shoulder where the hill drops away to the valley of the River Cock. They were large armies and they covered a lot of ground. The night of the 28th was bitterly cold. Doubtless both sides made fires where they could find enough fuel. Some men would stand around them; others would huddle themselves in their cloaks and pack tightly together, getting some sleep; for they were tired, and a hard man can sleep in almost any conditions, even in torrential rain, if he is weary and accustomed to such rigours. When they woke up, many of them were covered with snowflakes, and they would stamp around to get warm.

There was probably little food, for both armies were large, and the fact that we know next to nothing of medieval commissariat arrangements suggests that they were fairly scanty. But even with empty stomachs and cold hands morale on both sides was still high. It may seem strange that it should be so, but in medieval battle a man had the great comfort of seeing his own side, and its apparently superior numbers; and if he did not already believe the enemy were outnumbered and outclassed his commanders would undoubtedly tell him that it was so. It was only when he found later that the enemy also seemed to have unlimited numbers that he began to feel less confident. But then it was too late to think about it. There was no retreat. All he could do was to try to kill as many of them as he could, and hope his comrades were being as successful. Once the battle was joined he would not have time to be afraid. Neither side could see much of the other as they deployed at Towton. The snow was now blowing in gusts. Even if visibility had been good it is unlikely that either would have taken much note of the shallow gully in the ground separating the two armies. It sloped towards the River Cock and, later, when the armies were surging crowds of fighting men, it gradually tilted them towards the river itself.

Both armies were drawn up in two parallel lines on a wide front – some said it was as long as a mile, though this seems unlikely – with the archers to the fore and the infantry and men-at-arms behind. Command of the Lancastrian army was given to the Duke of Somerset; unlike his unpopular ancestor, he managed to survive a crucial battle. He also commanded the centre, which included Lord Dacre, who was less lucky. The Lancastrian right wing was commanded by the Earl of Northumberland; subsequently he escaped from the battlefield but died of his wounds at York. Exeter, who commanded the Lancastrian left, escaped and survived. However, it was clear from subsequent events that the left flank was badly positioned.

Opposite, the Yorkist left was commanded by Edward. Although only nineteen he was six foot four, and strong in proportion. He was untiring, and moved over the battlefield constantly encouraging. The centre was commanded by the resourceful Fauconberg, and the right by Warwick. Who would have thought that day that ten years later Warwick would lose his own life fighting for the opposite side at Barnet, and would lose it because once again he had abandoned his horse to show that there was no possibility that he would leave the field prematurely?

The Yorkists, as the challengers, advanced slowly to give battle. The wind was behind them and the snow over their heads was blowing into the Lancastrian faces. As the Yorkists came into range they loosed off the first flights of their arrows. They flighted them high into the wind and they flew over a broad front among Somerset's men. There would have been no chance of avoiding them even if they had not been obscured by the snowstorm but the fact that the snow was full of arrows was disconcerting. The Lancastrians replied hastily but as they launched their arrows blindly into the oncoming snowflakes the Yorkists had begun to fall back. Luck favoured the Yorkists for they were at extreme range when they loosed their arrows and now the Lancastrian arrows were falling short in no-man's land. It was a typical Fauconberg manoeuvre. He was a tactician to his finger-tips, a soldier who had learnt from every moment of battle experience. As the Lancastrian arrows fell short he ordered his men to gather them up and send them back. By this time the Lancastrian arrows were running short and it must have seemed as if they were facing an army of archers. Arrows were a great asset but were soon gone; when that had happened an archer became a lightly-armed foot soldier, and highly vulnerable unless he was following up a successful arrow attack. However, the Lancastrians were not easily upset, and when the two sides began close-quarter fighting the slaughter among the lightly-armoured archers was very high indeed. Here men fought as they had fought at Agincourt, climbing over piles of dead bodies to get at the enemy. It was kill or be killed, but more often kill *and* be killed. This was one of several 'bloody meadows' which marked the battlefield. Local names usually show the more intense areas of fighting and 'bloody meadows' and 'red pieces' are found on many an ancient map. Towton seems to have had at least two: one where the two forward lines clashed in the hollow, and another to the left where the fighting swayed down towards the flooded river. The fighting in this quarter went on relentlessly all through the morning. Clearly there must have been pauses for breath but these did not last long. When a party of men from either side were victorious they looked around for fresh victims. The battle was not now being fought on a basis of tactics ordered by commanders, but was a huge desperate horde of men, fully committed to battle, past fear but not past revenge and hatred. Victory, they knew, would come only when the other side had been killed or had fled. The armies were so huge, and it was so difficult to get at the other side that large numbers still remained uncommitted as the battle continued hour after hour.

The turning-point seems to have occurred in the early afternoon, and, ironically, because the latecomers put in their appearance. It seems that Norfolk, who had been sent to collect his retainers and make them into an army when Edward was still at London, had at last caught up with the battle. He arrived along the Ferry-bridge road and charged into the struggling mass which the battle had now become. It seems doubtful whether the Lancastrians can have recognized Norfolk's men as fresh troops but the shock of their charge into the right flank of the battle must have gradually pushed the whole conflict down the slope towards the River Cock. That slope is very steep in parts and once a man found himself on it he would not be able to check himself until he reached the bottom. And at the bottom were the flooded meadows of the river. Many Lancastrians, realizing that the battle was lost, now tried to cross those marshes and the stream itself. But the stream, already full of rain and snow, was soon blocked with bodies, and overflowed its banks. Anyone trying to cross it would be supremely lucky if he were not drowned. It would have been difficult enough to cross, encumbered as they were, without wounds or harassing Yorkists. It is not surprising to learn that the waters ran red with blood for six miles.

Some of those from the Lancastrian left and centre tried to fall back, and then to flee, to the town of Tadcaster. There again they met the river, and here, on Somerset's orders, the bridge had been destroyed before the battle. Again there was soon a bridge of dead bodies in the ford but here the Yorkist cavalry were able to enjoy themselves among the Lancastrian fugitives caught in the open. Doubtless the Lancastrians were as cruel and ruthless themselves, but it is interesting to note that Wenlock, who with his men did great execution at Tadcaster, had his own brains scattered with an axe ten years later at Tewkesbury.

The Dacre memorial on what was once the Lancastrian centre may well mark the approximate spot where he was killed. It is related that in the height of the battle he took off his helmet in order to drink, and was shot by a boy who had hidden himself in the branches of an elder tree. The young archer recognized the hated badge of Dacre and made no mistake. There are no elder bushes around the memorial, which is now on plough, but there are plenty further along towards the river. Dacre was buried, on his horse, in a tomb in Saxton churchyard, and the tomb is still there to be seen. The inscriptions are now very difficult to read but described him as 'a true soldier and strenuous in war'. The churchyard was once filled with graves of the slain, but after five hundred years there is little trace of these or the numerous grave-pits which once marked the battlefield.

The battle lasted from dawn till dusk that bitter Palm Sunday, and doubtless many of both sides died on the following days as well. It was a decisive battle, and after it Edward was king until he became careless and temporarily lost his throne eight years later. But the hatreds of Towton were not purged on the battle-field. Many leading Lancastrians were subsequently caught and executed. Edward himself took down his father's head from the gate of York and replaced it with a number of Lancastrians'.

It was, of course, an epic or an appalling struggle, depending on which way you care to look at it. The pity of it was that the bravest and most enterprising men in the country should meet in what was such a suicidal battle. The loss was not merely Lancastrian or Yorkist but to the country as a whole.

THE BATTLES OF
HEDGELEY MOOR and HEXHAM

25 April 1464 • 15 May 1464

After Towton it might have been thought that there would be no
more Lancastrians capable of bearing arms, or, at least, willing
to do so. But there were. Not much was seen of them for a while
after Towton but gradually, as it was seen that young Edward
was more interested in drinking, gaudy clothes, and women than
in government, the Lancastrians took heart and decided that it
must have been by sheer luck that this dissipated fop had won
those great victories at Mortimer's Cross and Towton. Had
Edward exerted himself immediately to stamp out the last traces
of Lancastrian resistance the Wars of the Roses could have been
over then and there. But he did not. Instead he handed over all
the administration to his cousin, the Earl of Warwick. Warwick
was an extraordinary character. As a youth he had shown enough
initiative to win the first Battle of St Albans for the Yorkists. Subsequently he had proved himself a great military leader. Now he
was trying to show that he was not only a fine soldier in the field
but also a wise and popular statesman. (Later he would become
thwarted and revengeful, but that time was not yet.) In the years
after 1461, Warwick, who was enormously wealthy in his own
right, seemed to be trying to show that if he himself had been king
the country would have been the happier and better for it. He
captured the key northern castles of Bamburgh, Dunstanburgh,
and Alnwick, but relaxed his vigilance too soon and they were
twice lost in risings which were reinforced by Scots and French.
He – and Edward – clearly underestimated Margaret, who was

a remarkable person; married to a husband who was useless to her and often opposed her, and defeated time and again in battle and diplomacy, she never lost heart or allowed her resolution to be checked. She had many narrow escapes from death or capture. After Towton she was a penniless fugitive and once she, Henry VI, and the young Prince had lived on a herring a day between the three of them, for five days. The herring was all they had; there was no bread or anything else to eat. Several times she was captured by robbers; and on more than one occasion lucky not to have been murdered. It was not until Tewkesbury (1471) that at last she had to acknowledge defeat. By that time, most of the Lancastrian leaders had died in battle or by execution.

In 1461, in spite of Towton, Margaret was still full of fight. In 1464 she had managed to subvert all those northern Lancastrians who had been pardoned by Edward. Edward had known all the time that there was potential danger in the north, and had rather ingeniously contrived to sign truces with both Scotland and France which would hold good during 1464 – until October at least. While these were in force Edward planned a campaign to crush all further resistance in the north. He did not, of course, trust either France or Scotland but he considered that they would hardly wish to do more than help his enemies secretly, and that would mean on a minor scale. He then put his armies under the command of Lord Montagu, Warwick's younger brother. Both Warwick and his brother would be killed at Barnet seven years later, fighting for the Lancastrians against Edward. Such were the twists, turns, and treacheries of the Wars of the Roses.

While Edward was planning to demolish the last shreds of Lancastrian resistance, the Lancastrians had their own plans, and they boded ill for Edward. In April 1464, the Lancastrians mustered two small armies in Northumberland, where they still held the vital northern castles. Their number was not large but, as Edward very well knew, if they had a few initial successes recruits would pour in and the result of Towton might be reversed. The situation therefore looked ominous when the Lancastrians seized two vital strategic castles: Norham in Northumberland,

and Skipton in Yorkshire. Unfortunately for the Lancastrians they did not then push ahead with recruiting fast enough. Montagu therefore reached Durham without serious check, although Sir Ralph Percy tried to ambush him. Montagu heard of the plan and changed his route. Then, having obtained reinforcements at Newcastle, he set out to confront the Lancastrians. The battle which followed, vital though it was in this Northern campaign, has been very scantily chronicled but we know that Montagu had a well-balanced force of about 2000 and met the Lancastrian army at Hedgeley Moor, south-east of Wooler. The Lancastrians were in slight disarray at his sudden arrival. Apparently, supreme command had not been allotted, but the various detachments were under Lord Hungerford, Lord Ros (or Roos), and Sir Ralph Percy. The two former, realizing they were heavily out-numbered, soon saw excellent reasons why they should leave the field and fight another day, but Sir Ralph, as became a Percy, was made of sterner stuff. The Lancastrians then closed around Percy, whose force consisted mainly of his own tenants and retainers, and attempted to kill or capture all of them. Percy, how-ever, thought otherwise and made a spirited charge at what seemed the weakest part of the Yorkist line. At this point his horse made a tremendous jump – at what subsequently became known as 'Percy's Leap' – but was wounded shortly afterwards. Percy, too, received a wound and died quickly. His dying cry was 'I have saved the bird in my bosom' which is interpreted as meaning he had died for his lawful monarch, after temporarily deserting him when pardoned by Edward IV. His soldiers were methodically despatched by the Yorkists, mainly on the marshy part of the battlefield.*

A point, which brings out the complexity and folly of these wars, was that Percy's mother was a Neville. He was the seventh of her nine sons. The elder branch of the Neville family, who held the title of Earls of Westmorland, were staunch Lancastrians, and had always been so since Henry IV had taken the throne from

---

*The 'cross' is merely a stone column today. It is engraved with the arms of Percy and Lucy.

Richard II. But the younger branch of the Neville family, which was the line of the Earls of Warwick and the Earls of Salisbury, were equally staunch Yorkists (until, of course, Warwick 'the Kingmaker' changed sides shortly before his death in 1471). Whether the older and younger branches of the Neville family fought on opposite sides because of political sympathies, or whether because they were intense and bitter rivals and could not possibly have supported the same cause, is not known, but the latter seems more likely than the former.

So Percy was dead, and that was a bitter blow to the Lancastrians, but they had endured bitter blows before and still come back. Hope now resided in the Duke of Somerset, son of the unpopular minister who had been killed at the first battle of St Albans. Doubtless Montagu would have proceeded to battle straight away if he had known where to find the Lancastrians, but he did not. For the moment he could only move tentatively towards Bamburgh; then suddenly he heard that Somerset was with a substantial force at Hexham. Where Montagu himself was at the time is not precisely known but it was probably well to the north, for he did not reach Hexham till 14 May.

Somerset, who would be executed after this battle, had done everything to deserve it. After Towton he had been pardoned and then much favoured by Edward. He was made custodian of Bamburgh Castle and captain of the royal guard. Edward gave him money, though he had not too much himself, and saw that Somerset's titles and estates were restored to him. Somerset was less popular with others and, when the two had visited Northampton, Somerset had nearly been killed; Edward saved his unpopular friend's life only by distributing so much wine that the crowd of would-be assassins were too drunk to know where to look. He then sent Somerset to North Wales for his own safety.

But Somerset had wearied of the royal friendship and seemed hell-bent on his own destruction. First he assembled as many Lancastrian supporters as he could find in North Wales and then rode with them one night through the Yorkist lines to Newcastle. Edward reacted much more quickly than Somerset had expected,

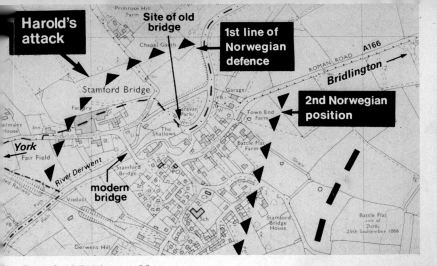

I   Stamford Bridge, 1066

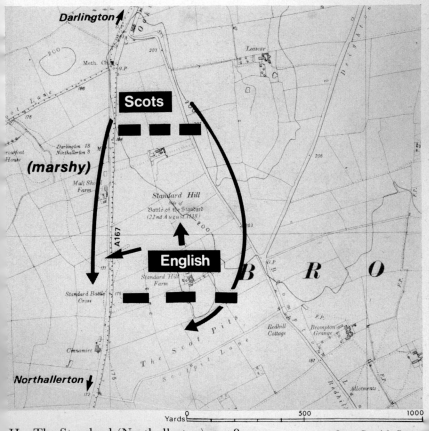

II   The Standard (Northallerton), 1138

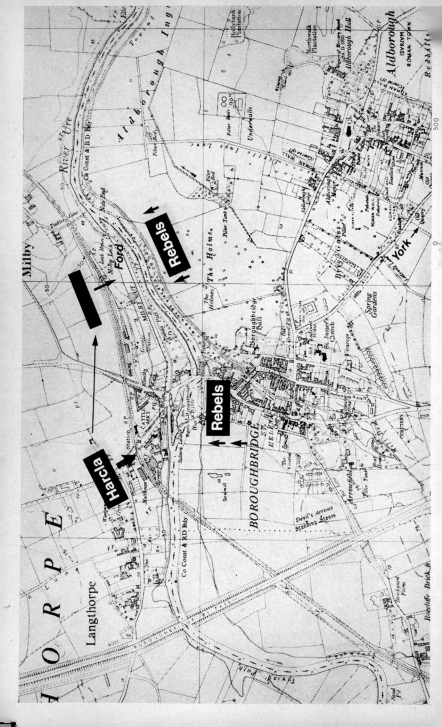

Langthorpe

Milby

Rebels

Ford

Harcia

Rebels

BOROUGHBRIDGE

Aldborough

ISVRIVM
ROMAN TOWN

York

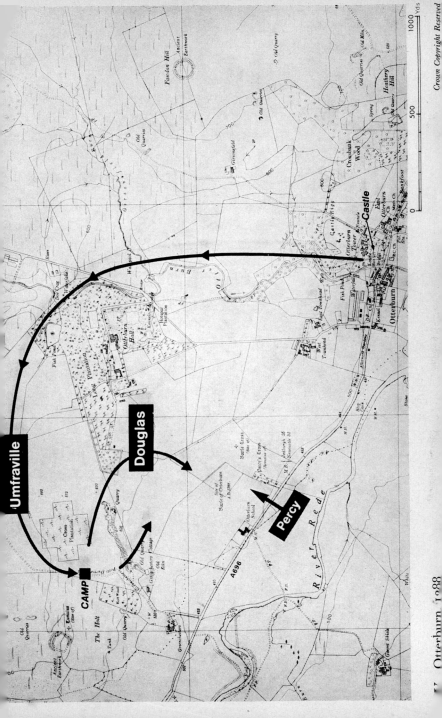

Umfraville

Douglas

Percy

CAMP

Castle

Otterburn

Faelon Hill

Heathery Hill

River Rede

A696

7 Otterburn 1388

1000 Yds

500

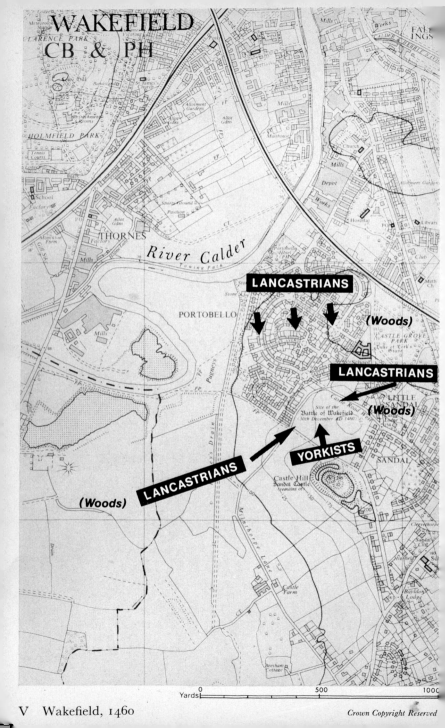

V   Wakefield, 1460

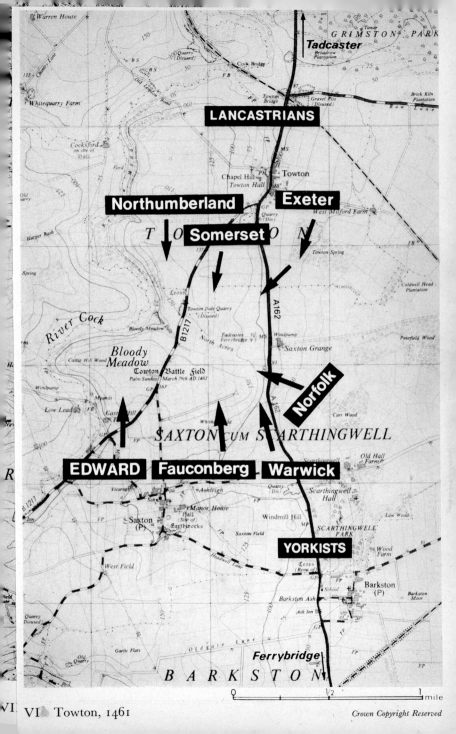

Tadcaster

GRIMSTON PARK

LANCASTRIANS

Towton

Northumberland

Exeter

Somerset

River Cock

B1217

A162

Bloody Meadow

Towton Battle Field
Palm Sunday March 29th AD 1461

Norfolk

SAXTON cum SCARTHINGWELL

EDWARD   **Fauconberg**   **Warwick**

Saxton
(P)

SCARTHINGWELL
PARK

YORKISTS

Barkston
(P)

Ferrybridge

B A R K S T O N

0   1/2   1 mile

VI Towton, 1461

Crown Copyright Reserved

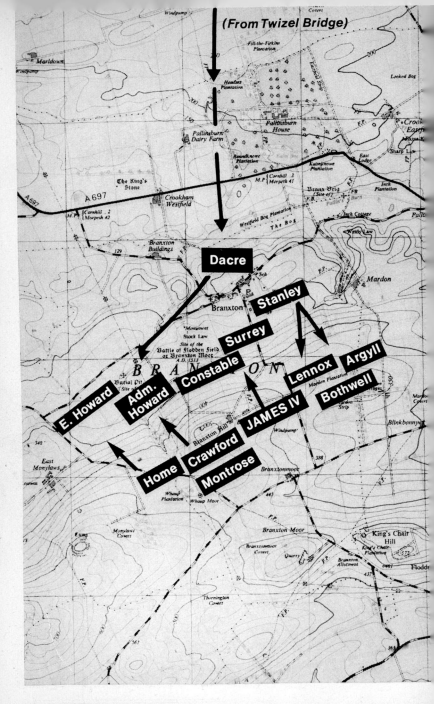

IX Flodden, 1513

(To Twizel Bridge 4½ m. approx.)

Route of English Army

0   ½   1   2 mile

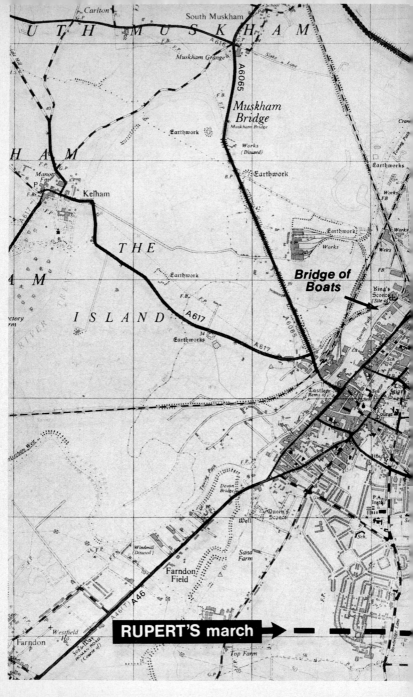

X Newark, 1644

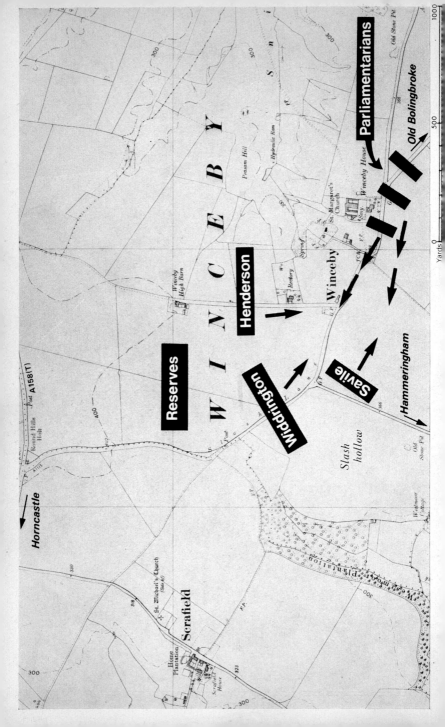

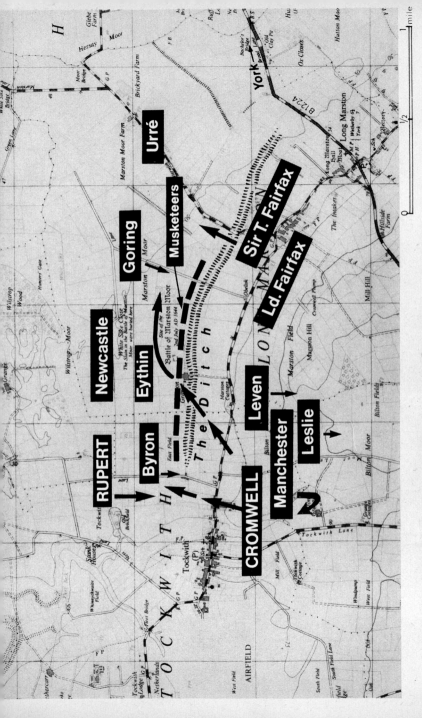

XII Marston Moor, 1644

XIII   Preston, 1648

PARLIAMENTARIANS

Langdale

Crown Copyright Reserved

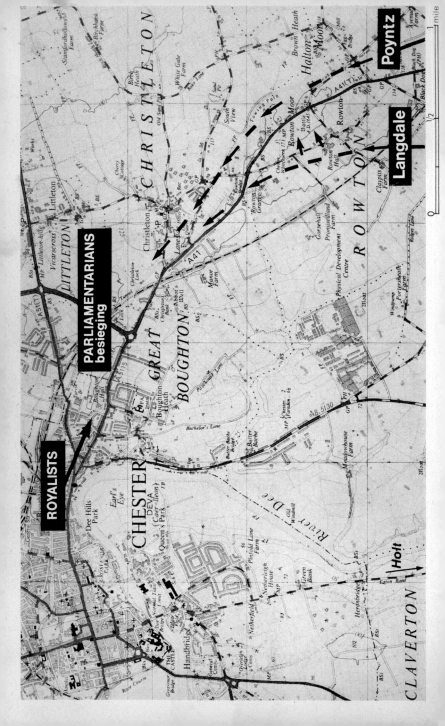

POYNTZ

PARLIAMENTARIANS
besieging

LANGDALE

ROYALISTS

CHRISTLETON

ROWTON

GREAT
BOUGHTON

CHESTER
DEVA
(Caer-lleon)

LITTLETON

CLAVERTON

Holt

seized Newcastle, and executed Somerset's men. Somerset had meanwhile moved to Bamburgh.

In hindsight it is all crystal clear. When not fighting, Edward was so casual, debauched, and apparently incompetent, that no one could believe he was secure on the throne. The incident at Northampton must have convinced Somerset that Edward was only hanging on to his power by a mere thread. He was not the only one to make such miscalculations. In peace, Edward was a self-indulgent fop; in danger, he was alert, indefatigable, and brilliant at both strategy and tactics. Somerset was soon to learn this at the cost of his own life.

Hedgeley Moor had been a setback but, owing to their prudence – or cowardice – in leaving the field early, the Lancastrian strength had not been greatly diminished. In the ensuing three weeks Somerset busied himself with enlisting every possible Lancastrian supporter; doubtless the promise of rewards did not err on the side of restraint. On 14 May he arrived at Hexham and pitched camp at Linnels, on the banks of the Devilswater. It was a good place for a camp but a bad place for a battle. Somerset's army had its backs to a curve in the stream at Hexham Levels, his front was screened by a wooded hill. It was unlikely that he could be surprised, for the Devilswater was a fast stream and just to the right of his position it was joined by the West Dipton Burn which would be very difficult to cross. It was as snug a camp as you could wish for, and well protected by natural features. However, it was distinctly less satisfactory when an army approached, as Somerset soon found; but he had the sense to dispose his forces well forward in the face of Montagu's oncoming army, and thus gave himself some space to manoeuvre on either side. He had also been wise enough to leave Henry at Bywell Castle and not to risk such a valuable hostage – or encumbrance – on the battlefield.

Montagu, once he learnt of Somerset's position, came up at great speed, hoping to pin the Lancastrians against the river and cramp any possible manoeuvres. This type of tactic is excellent provided your own men are going to be superior in the inevitable close-quarter fighting. If, however, the opposition fight with the desperation of the doomed, it may be necessary to order a fast retreat and quick regroup, for the battle may be lost on minor tactics. In the event, Montagu was lucky, for the Lancastrians were on a broad front, and the wings, seeing the centre yielding, did not reinforce it but themselves took to flight. In the general confusion of Lancastrians fanning out in several directions at once, some men from the centre had the time necessary to cross the Devilswater and escape. As was seen at Towton and elsewhere, crossing a stream was a possibility, if you had time and were unhampered, but was a death-trap if the pursuers were close at your back. Somerset was wounded, was slower at getting away than some of the others, and was captured about a mile from the battlefield. He was taken into Hexham and executed with the greatest indignity. His spurs were struck off by a common servitor, his coat of arms was torn off, and he was strapped to a hurdle. Then he was dragged to the scaffold and beheaded.

It was only one of many executions. Ros and Hungerford were also captured and were beheaded at Newcastle. Other Lancastrian leaders were executed at various points, some as far south as York, to convince potential Lancastrian supporters that allegiance to Henry VI and Queen Margaret was a quick way to the scaffold. However, Henry had been warned, and had escaped, though leaving all his personal possessions behind him, including his sword. The great northern Lancastrian strongholds, Alnwick, Dunstanburgh, Norham, and Bamburgh surrendered soon afterwards, though the last-named required gunfire to make it haul down its flag. With that the Lancastrian cause in the north was ended for the time being.

THE BATTLE OF FLODDEN

9 September 1513

The last chapter ended with the complete defeat of the Lancastrians in 1464. In this account we describe a devastating victory in the reign of a king who was born of the union of a Lancastrian king and a Yorkist queen. The intervening events and reasons may be sketched in very rapidly. More detailed accounts of the battles involved are to be found in the other books of this 'British Battlefields' series but, as they did not take place in the north, can be treated only incidentally in this volume.

All would have been well for Edward if he had not rather foolishly married a Lancastrian widow, Elizabeth Woodville, and made no attempt to mollify those of his supporters who felt affronted by the match. Chief among the aggrieved was Warwick, but Edward's response was only to try to humiliate the great 'Kingmaker' who seemed to him altogether too powerful and influential. Warwick thereupon allied himself with Edward's younger brother, the Duke of Clarence, and organized a rebellion in 1469 which resulted in the Battle of Edgecote and the capture of Edward himself. Edward was subsequently released on parole but, inevitably, took the first opportunity to raise an army and chase Warwick and Clarence out of the country. Burning with humiliation and rage, Warwick offered his services to Margaret who was then living in exile in France. But this uneasy alliance caused nothing but further bloodshed. Warwick himself was killed at Barnet (1471) and, in the same year, Margaret was imprisoned after the Battle of Tewkesbury where her son and heir had been killed (or perhaps murdered after the battle). Henry VI also died mysteriously at this time, in the Tower of London, probably with the assistance of his gaolers.

However, after twelve years, Edward's way of life had changed him from a superbly fit young man into a debauched invalid; he died at the age of forty-one. By then he had had ten children by his lawful wife and an unspecified number by mistresses.

The new heir was Edward V, who subsequently became one of the two princes who disappeared without trace in the Tower of London. The next king was Richard of Gloucester, who became Richard III. His reign was short; having taken the throne in 1483 he was killed at Bosworth in 1485.

Henry VII, who had an extremely easy and lucky campaign to obtain the throne in 1485, married the late King Edward IV's eldest daughter. At long last the rivalry between the factions of Lancaster and York was now dissolved by a dynastic marriage. What was rather more to the point was that nearly all the potential trouble-makers had killed each other or been executed during the previous thirty years. Furthermore, the country was as anxious for peace as Henry was to provide it. This did not entirely prevent battles, as was seen at Stoke Field in 1487, Britanny in 1491, and Blackheath in 1497, but it did eventually produce stability, a full treasury, and a docile aristocracy.

But Henry VII's successor was of different mettle entirely. The young Henry VIII – he was only eighteen when he succeeded – was very able, quite ruthless, and a heavy spender. Furthermore, he was always anxious to prove that he was better than others. Success seemed to come naturally to him, and he was also very lucky. In 1513 he landed at Calais with an army of 25,000 men. After capturing two towns with very little effort he won the 'Battle of the Spurs'. The battle took its name from the haste with which the French knights urged their horses from the contest.

While Henry was thus engaged, the Scots, who were distinctly fonder of the French than the English, decided that the time was ripe to settle a few outstanding military accounts. Fortunately for England, Henry had left the country in charge of Thomas

Howard, Earl of Surrey. Howard was no youngster; he had even fought for Richard III against Henry VII at Bosworth. Subsequently he had been pardoned and proved a loyal servant of the new king, who had appointed him Lord Lieutenant of the North. Surrey did not at first realize that this was to be full-scale war but after a very large raiding party, under the Earl of Home, had been ambushed, it seemed to him that the Scots were intent on more than border raiding. He therefore briskly set about the organization of a suitable defensive army. This was early in August 1513. The muster point was Newcastle. There converged an interesting motley of forces, and Surrey took to it the banner of St Cuthbert which was alleged to be the one carried against the Scots at Neville's Cross 167 years before, and was doubtless believed to be the same one that was taken by Thurstan to Northallerton in 1138, 375 years before. Like Thurstan, Surrey was too crippled to take part in the fighting – he was over seventy – and travelled to the battle by coach. However, Surrey scarcely needed propaganda to boost his efforts; he was well-experienced in the art of war and had the measure of James IV. On being sure that James was intent on a full-scale invasion he sent him a challenge. The significance of a challenge went back to medieval times, and its chivalric implication was that the acceptor would fight at the date and place named. Surrey hoped that this challenge would cause the Scots to fight on ground unsuitable to them. It did not, however, work out quite as well as that, for James was no fool and had taken up position at Flodden Edge. It was said that he had 100,000 men. The number was probably a third of that amount. James had plenty of men and some useful arms, including 600 hand culverins* and 400 arquebuses, but his force was undisciplined and insufficiently trained. His men also had 6000 pikes, but handling a pike, which can be up to eighteen feet long, in formation requires time and practice. An untrained pikeman is a bigger danger to his own side than to the enemy.

Heavier artillery consisted of five large cannon, each of which

---

*Culverin is another name for a cannon and derives from the French word coulevrine(=snake).

required a team of oxen (seven) to draw it, and twelve culverins of varying sizes. Cannons were very effective, when they functioned properly, but usually produced endless problems. In 1460, at the siege of Roxburgh, James II of Scotland had been killed when one of his own cannons burst, and at all times early cannon were unreliable. Their explosive charge was usually too violent, which made them dangerous and erratic, or too slow-burning, which made them ineffective. Ammunition was a problem, too, for whereas the old siege catapults had been highly effective with almost any lump of stone, and quite accurate as well, cannon-balls had to be carefully shaped, and therefore took time to prepare. This could rarely be done near the battlefield; there was therefore the need for an enormous ammunition train. Nevertheless, when the cannons and culverins started peppering castle walls the effect on morale was even greater than the effect on the masonry. Thus Wark, Norham, Chillingham, and Etall castles surrendered to the Scots much more quickly than they needed to have done, particularly the last.

Surrey took his army to Wooler in two divisions. It numbered approximately 25,000 but there were another 50,000 available in the midlands and south who might come up and join him if for some reason it was decided to delay the confrontation with the Scots. Larger numbers in that area might have proved more of an embarrassment than an asset, for food supplies were distinctly meagre in the border area. Surrey had less artillery than the Scots but more archers. He also had 1000 marines brought in by his son Admiral Henry Howard, who was his second-in-command. At Wooler the English army was only six miles from the invader.

However, it would have been extremely foolish of Surrey to have challenged the Scots in their strong position. It was a pity that they had refused his challenge and declined to face him on ground of his own choosing; this unsporting, unmedieval decision was blamed on the French who were present with James and undoubtedly advising him. However, this being so, it was necessary to tempt or frighten the Scots out of their position if that were possible.

With extraordinary boldness (or rashness, depending on how

you look on these matters) Surrey ordered his army to march due north from Wooler on 8 September. It was pouring with rain at the time and the tracks were full of water and mud. Surrey was taking almost every risk it is possible to take. He was presenting a long flank to the enemy, and at the end of his march, although he would be between the Scots and their homeland, equally well he had placed his own army between a large invasion army and its hostile motherland. The journey involved his crossing the River Till, using the bridge at Twizel and the Milford ford. Although it is not exactly known it seems likely that they moved dismounted, as under those conditions the horses would have been too much of a liability. Apparently they had had no beer for days and they accomplished that march without food either. Once across the river the army veered back to the south.

The move took the Scots by surprise but did not have precisely the effect intended. Instead of descending to the plain the Scots moved north to the other edge of the ridge, which is known as Branxton Hill, and took up positions facing northwards. The slope is steep here, being about one in five. The highest point is Pipers Hill and at the bottom of the slope lies a boggy area known as Pallinsburn. Like many bogs this varies somewhat in firmness from one year to another, but extends over approximately a mile. There were only two reasonable crossing-places, one being at Branx Brig, the other at Sandyford. The English army had taken the precaution of obtaining a local guide and Admiral Howard's division proceeded to cross at Branx Brig while Surrey's took the ford. As they came out of the water, which lay on the surface, they saw the Scottish army ahead of them on the ridge. It was in four solid detachments, each about 200 yards apart. In between could be seen the Scottish artillery. The entire frontage was about 2000 yards. As the English came closer they came into range of the heavier guns – about 1500 yards – but the few shots fired at this stage buried themselves harmlessly in the bog. It was a delicate moment, for the two divisions of the English army, Admiral Howard's and the Earl of Surrey's, were well out of touch; had the Scots charged down the hill on to Howard's advance column

Flodden might have had a very different result. However, James IV had no information about the disposition of the English army, and could scarcely guess it was in such a vulnerable state. Meanwhile, Howard halted and Surrey was able to close up. The opportunity was lost. Nevertheless, no one could blame the Scots for not abandoning such an excellent position. The Admiral must have sweated gently as he realized that about a mile separated the two sections of the English army. However, he was not too apprehensive to note that the Scottish army was in four columns, while the English was in six. Should one or more of those columns come down the hill they might punch a hole in the English front which would be irreparable. It was now the afternoon of the 9th, and the English spent it in reforming so that the Scottish squares opposite were as nearly matched as the disparity in numbers allowed. And it was still raining.

As the two armies faced each other, now only 600 yards apart, the artillery opened up. Visibility was naturally very poor, and as a result the Scottish artillery over-ranged. The English artillery, inferior in size and numbers, were fortuitously presented with an advantage. Having no facility of range they simply discharged point blank into what was their only possible target area. It was, of course, crowded with Scottish infantry. Goaded into desperation, the left flank of the Scottish army, on to which most of the rounds were falling, decided to charge forward. These were not disciplined troops, accustomed to holding their effort till the last moment; they were wild Borderers, second to none in offensive spirit, but completely unaccustomed to fighting in an army with an essential pattern of disciplined commitment. As they came down the hill they looked even more formidable than they were. But they were powerful enough, too, and they tore through Howard's division, killing many and putting more to flight. It was a fine start to the battle from the Scottish point of view but not quite as good as it looked. The English right had not been entirely demolished; it only seemed to be so. But to James IV, seeing it from the top of the hill it looked like the prelude to absolute victory: up to this point the Scots had decided that nothing would tempt them from their commanding position on the hilltop; now it seemed that a full-scale attack on to the wilting English army would rapidly bring immediate victory. James launched his own column, and the adjoining one (under Crawford and Montrose). They tore down the hill, crossed the stream at the bottom, and came up a slight slope to the English line.

But a charge up a slope of 200 yards can take the edge off the most enthusiastic warrior. Although Surrey's men were pushed back they were not scattered, and soon the Scottish drive forward had stopped. At that point the Borderers should have added their weight to the Scottish attack. Two factors prevented this: one was that the Borderers had lost whatever cohesion they had had once they put their opposites to rout; the second was that Lord Dacre was waiting in reserve with 1500 cavalry behind the English lines. On seeing the havoc created by the Borderers, but at the same time noting their vulnerability, he brought his men smartly forward into the Borderers' flank. On that wing, therefore, there was now a confused mass of struggling men. Whatever happened, that locked-up mass could hardly have any further effect on the battle. But there were plenty of others, on both sides, who could.

They were, of course, on the Scottish right wing and the English left. The division on the right of the Scottish centre was commanded by King James himself, the right wing by the Earls of Argyll and Lennox. There was also a reserve commanded by the Earl of Bothwell which contained some French men-at-arms. Opposite King James was the Earl of Surrey, so the two commanders-in-chief were directly opposed. Surrey's division contained at least 3000 Yorkshiremen and numbered about 5000 altogether. On his left was a division, also numbering 5000, commanded by Sir Edward Stanley. It was composed of men from Lancashire and Cheshire.

King James's men charged vigorously into Surrey's division as the latter was ascending the Branxton slope. James had armed himself with a pike and was in the front rank, but before his division had covered the 300 yards to the English line it had lost a good number of men to accurate cannon-fire and archery. When the two forces closed, the English bills, which were shorter than the Scottish pikes, proved a good deal more manoeuvrable. Finding their long pikes – to which they were unaccustomed – far too cumbersome, the Scots abandoned them and resorted to lighter weapons. This was unwise, for their swords were considerably shorter than the English bills, and much less effective.

Meanwhile, the extreme right of the Scottish army had been held in reserve. Their inactivity had been noted by Stanley who decided to give them a surprise. Under cover of the rain and mist he was able to move around to his left unobtrusively, and then, taking advantage of a gulley, to come up the hill unobserved. When they appeared they were at close quarters to the Highlanders opposing them, and announced their presence with several well-directed flights of arrows. Surprise at their unexpected appearance, and inability to retaliate to the well-directed arrows, had a devastating effect on the Highlanders. Unable to get within range, they fell back. Inevitably they were soon colliding with the front ranks of Bothwell's reserve detachment, and the English following up were able to pick easy targets in the general confusion. Bothwell himself was killed. In this quarter at least, the battle bore a close resemblance to the Battle of the Standard. Perhaps the spirit of old Thurstan, as well as that of St Cuthbert, was presiding over the scene. The Scots in this division were so undisciplined that they busied themselves looting their own dead rather than setting about the English. It did them little good, for they were soon chopped down by Stanley's men.

As this part of the Scottish army gave little resistance, Stanley's men soon turned round and charged down the slope again into the other fighting. Here, around James IV, were the *élite* of the Scottish army, worthy of better support than their flanks had given them. The fighting in this sector was bitter and long. James IV was killed, but the fighting went on. Only as night fell did the task seem hopeless and the Scots respond to the call to abandon fighting. Many, of course, did not do so but took a chance on finding a way back to Scotland. Casualties had been high on both sides in this part of the field. The final casualty lists were said to include 12,000 Scots and 4000 English.

Much discussion has gone on as to how the Scots, with an advantage of artillery, position, and numbers, could have lost this bloody battle. It is not difficult to find a reasonable explanation. The Scottish army, although large, consisted of largely untrained troops, who were therefore undisciplined. Although well armed, they did not know how to use their arms, let alone how to fight in formation with them. It is perhaps possible to exaggerate this point, for the Scots threw away their new acquisitions when they found they were unable to make good use of them, but the effect on morale of finding that an alleged winning weapon was merely a liability was undoubtedly enormous. The Scottish army was also badly handled; brave though James IV was, he had no business to be fighting in the front ranks of an army he was supposed to be commanding. His subordinate commanders appear to have been of inferior quality. One of them, the Earl of Home, who commanded the Borderers on the left wing, was subsequently executed for inactivity amounting to treachery during the battle. He had apparently agreed with Dacre that their men would no longer continue fighting each other, although it was obvious that there was much to be done both in this sector and elsewhere. Whether the charge was justified or not seems doubtful; there had to be a scapegoat and Home was the best one to hand.

Had James IV won the battle instead of losing it there would doubtless have been high praise for his tactical skill in choosing such an excellent position, his prudence in not abandoning it in the face of English provocation, and his inspired dash to attack the English just when they were at their most vulnerable.

The explanation of the result is always seen more easily from the victor's viewpoint. Surrey's army was lean, hungry, and fit. They had everything to fight for. By contrast the Scots had done little to make them battle-fit. In fact, their forages had probably contributed to the reverse effect. When the English finally entered their camp they found it full of comforts, including large quantities of mutton, beer, and wine. Good rations make a man fight well if he is well-exercised but can have a very bad effect if he is not.

Surrey and Howard were capable commanders; Dacre and Stanley were soldiers with the touch of enterprise which usually brings complete disaster or complete victory. At Flodden they brought victory.

Described as above, the Battle of Flodden probably seems a very clear-cut affair. Needless to say, it was undoubtedly the exact opposite on the field itself. As the English arrows sped home, horses panicked and companies of men surged to and fro. As the Scottish pike companies began to move, the rough ground caused them to lose their formation, and, when they closed, English and Scots became too closely mingled for anyone to know how the battle was going. Dacre's charge probably killed some of his own side who were unable to get out of the way; in the rain, the darkness, and the general confusion there must have been many a man who found he was fighting one of his own side, and found it out too late.

One view of the Scottish strategy which has never been put forward might tentatively be advanced here. When James realized that his left wing had run away with itself and was perhaps lost to the battle, and the right wing was of such doubtful quality that it was only worth committing as expendable or in the poised moment of victory, he might have decided that his only chance was to smash a way right through the centre of the English line. If he broke through at that point he could, if he wished, put himself on the way to Scotland, but even if that was not his intention he would have cut the English army in half; his wings could then roll down the slope and complete the victory.

If that was his intention, it did not work. The English centre was too solid, and his impetus was lost even before he reached it. Instead of leading an advance therefore, he was caught in a desperate mêlée and killed. All other theories of the battle imply that he was a stupid field commander, but it could have been otherwise; unfortunately for the Scots the English stood a little too firm and the Scottish king and commander was killed. Perhaps, like many a general before and after him he was a good tactician but an unlucky general.

On Pipers Hill there is a memorial which was erected in 1910. Pipers Hill is about 100 yards from base to summit and has a gradient of about one in five from every angle. It was the scene of heavy fighting during which the ground became so slippery with blood that the surviving soldiers took off their boots to get a better foothold (or so it was said).

It seems that James refused to let the commander of his artillery open fire on the English before they had assembled after crossing the River Till because of the challenge to meet Surrey 'on a fair field'. James had spent the previous night at Ford Castle where his personal effects remained untouched until 1940.

THE BATTLE OF
WINCEBY

11 October 1643

On the Ordnance Survey map of Lincolnshire (no. 114 at 315 689) will be found the hamlet of Winceby. It is marked on the signposts on each side but there is no name by the roadside to indicate the place itself. However, if the visitor takes the A.158 from Horncastle and turns off to the A.115 for Spilsby he will come upon it 1¼ miles along the Spilsby road. If he reaches the turn to Old Bolingbroke, he has gone too far and must retrace his steps. There is a square-built Georgian house on the left of the road as he comes from Horncastle and that was doubtless the Roundhead headquarters. The Parliamentarian troops were drawn up in three divisions along the A.115 facing north, with Cromwell in the van, Fairfax in the centre, and Manchester in the rear. About half a mile further north another ridge crosses the road and on this the Royalists were drawn up in triangular formation, Savile on the right wing, Henderson on the left, and Widdrington to the centre. Why, in the autumn of 1643, some of the cream of English youth should be thus drawn up ready to slaughter each other requires some explanation.

The last battle described in this series – Flodden – had taken place a hundred and twenty years before. (There had, of course, been plenty of other battles involving English arms in the mean-time, but not in the area concerned in this book.) Flodden was the last of the medieval-type battles to be fought in this country and, after it, weapons and tactics changed completely. The bow disappeared from armies and was replaced by firearms. For many years firearms were less efficient than bows but they had the enormous advantage that they could be used by young and old with very little practice. The bow, on the other hand, needed incessant, lengthy practice and a good physique. A further point was that ammunition for firearms was much easier to transport. When bullets were effective they went right through armour so that even with erratic shooting it was inevitable that armour would now be discarded. And with the removal of heavy armour on both horse and man there was no longer need for the heavy draught-horse type of animal; instead, a lighter, faster mount took the field, and a whole complex of cavalry manoeuvres was evolved. However, after a time the popularity of the cavalry arm produced its own set of problems. Horses need forage, can go lame, fall ill, bolt, prove uncontrollable in battle. Born cavalrymen are not easily come by, and any sort of cavalrymen take some time to train.

All this had been taking place against a background of growing economic progress, and political development. When Henry VIII had broken with the Church of Rome and appointed himself head of the English church, monasteries had disappeared, church lands had passed into private hands, and the enclosure acts had begun to alter the appearance of the countryside. The reigns of Edward VI, Mary, and Elizabeth had seen this economic change continue and develop; they had also seen plots, some of which had led to full-scale battles, but nothing to compare with the destructive, internal rivalries of the past.

But in the middle of the seventeenth century England was once more torn apart by Civil War. It was not, however, a recurrence of the situation which had caused the Wars of the Roses but something entirely different, although no less suicidal. It was an altogether more complex matter. The people who made up the armies of the Civil War were not, as is often thought, people of similar views and aspirations, any more than today all those who vote Conservative are rich and privileged and all those who vote Socialist are poor and deprived. Then, as now, there were a host of different reasons which caused a man to side with one party or the other. Conscience undoubtedly played a large part but so also did tradition, regional affiliations, and temperament.

The Civil War probably became inevitable when Elizabeth died unmarried; for the next heir was James VI of Scotland who became James I of England. His personal qualities – or lack of them – made him a useless king but that in itself would not have mattered greatly. Unfortunately he possessed obsolete ideas on the power of the monarch, and brought up his son to share them. James believed that kings held their position by divine right, according to a strict hereditary law of succession. This had never been an English custom and, indeed, if it had been strictly adhered to James I would never have sat on the English throne at all. However, this crackbrained idea went with one that the king had a 'royal prerogative' which entitled him to ignore, or set on one side, any Parliamentary law of which he did not approve. Needless to say, his ideas led to a series of plots, some of which had obscure aims and peculiar adherents. The best known is the Gunpowder Plot of 1605 for which Guy Fawkes, and his fellow conspirators, were killed outright, or executed in a slower and more spectacular way.

By the time James I died, relations between king and Parliament were extremely poor, and an open breach had been prevented only by James's idleness and personal cowardice. However, when (in 1625) his son Charles succeeded him, hopes ran high. Here was an intelligent, courageous, and virtuous young man. It seemed that England was now set fair for a Golden Age. Unfortunately, it was on a course for a disastrous Civil War.

The stages by which this became inevitable do not concern us here. The Royal Standard was set up at Nottingham on 22 August 1642, and Charles invited all his supporters to rally to him there. Meanwhile Parliament appointed the Earl of Essex as commander-in-chief. Then followed nine years of virtually continuous war, although there was a short pause between 1647 and 1648. Needless to say, throughout this long suicidal contest both parties believed they were protecting the Constitution. Even the Parliamentarians believed that they were fighting for the true rights of the Crown. This, of course, was slightly offset by the fact that the Royalists believed that the Parliamentarians were a host of fanatical bigots and the Parliamentarians considered that the Royalist supporters –

and the king too – were not to be trusted. Broadly speaking, country districts supported Charles, and the towns, particularly on the eastern side of the country, supported Parliament. There were, of course, exceptions; it should be remembered that one third of the aristocracy supported Parliament. Unfortunately, close neighbours, friends, and even relations were divided in their sympathies.

The first battle, at Edgehill, was fought on 23 October 1642. It was inconclusive. Even so, Charles could have moved on to take London if he had been determined enough. Instead, he was deterred by the train-bands which opposed him at Turnham Green, and fell back to Reading. He offered peace to Parliament – on his terms – but when they rejected his offer, retired to Oxford. But while Charles was inactive there was plenty of fighting going on elsewhere. The result was that the Parliamentary forces gained control of the east and south, including most of the ports, while the north and west, including Wales but excepting the town (and port) of Pembroke, came under Royalist control. In the spring of 1643 local fighting was vigorous but not significant. The summer was more decisive and some important battles took place in the Midlands. Notable among them were Chalgrove Field (18 June 1643) in which Hampden was killed; Lansdown (5 July) when Waller's Parliamentary army was beaten by Hopton; and Roundway Down (13 July) when the Parliamentarians, now nicknamed 'Roundheads', were beaten again. The valuable port of Bristol was then captured by the Royalists. Now was the time for Charles to march on London, and take it, which he should have been able to do. Disastrously for his cause, he failed to make the move. It is said that he paid too much attention to local commanders who wished to consolidate the recent victories in their areas.

Instead, he suffered a setback which he could easily have avoided. It was caused by an attempt to be too clever strategically. Having taken Bristol, he decided it would be wise and timely to capture Gloucester, which was the only major port held by the Parliamentarians in the west. He began the siege on 10 August, but broke it off when Essex came from London with a powerful force, determined to relieve Gloucester at all costs. Charles, possibly over-influenced by cavalry opinion, decided not to fight in the siege-lines but to withdraw and manoeuvre to ambush Essex on the road back to London (after resupplying Gloucester). It was an interesting plan, but in the first Battle of Newbury, where the ambush took place, the execution went sadly wrong. The assumption that Essex's young, inexperienced train-bands would scatter and flee when subjected to a cavalry charge proved ill-founded, and at the end of the day it was the Royalist cavalry who had sustained most of the losses. Charles ordered his troops back to Oxford and the Roundheads were able to occupy Reading.

Meanwhile, a new figure had appeared on the scene in eastern England. This was Colonel Oliver Cromwell. Cromwell was not, as is often thought, a humble artisan who rose to high command for political reasons; on the contrary, he was a country gentleman with distinguished connections, and a thoroughly capable field commander who rose in rank through sheer merit. Not least of the reasons for his success was his insistence on the careful selection of all subordinate commanders. After Edgehill he criticized the Parliamentary army as consisting of 'old decayed serving-men and tapsters', but equally well he did not want people who thought that the accident of birth entitled them to command. What he wanted was the dash and courage of the young country gentleman combined with professional knowledge and enthusiasm, but with it a strong religious feeling which would temper a man in victory and sustain him in reverse.

By the autumn of 1643 Cromwell's views were beginning to show results. His cavalry had already proved itself in battle at Grantham and Gainsborough. Since June, Sir Thomas Fairfax and his son had been besieged by the Marquis of Newcastle in Hull. On 26 September Cromwell slipped across the Humber and took off Sir Thomas Fairfax. As Newcastle's army were so unvigilant as to let him do that he returned later and took off 500 cavalrymen as well.

Stung by this defiance, Newcastle took action to prove that he still held the initiative. An attempted Royalist coup in King's Lynn had been suppressed by the Earl of Manchester, and the latter moved towards the castle of Old Bolingbroke* – now in ruins, but then housing a substantial Royalist garrison. Bolingbroke was a Royalist outpost in a predominantly Parliamentarian area and it was as important to the prestige of the former to hold it as it was to the latter to reduce it. Manchester's peremptory order to the Royalists to surrender was defied with gusto, possibly because they knew that Newcastle had every intention of relieving them in the near future.

Newcastle moved south. The combined army which approached Bolingbroke was composed of three divisions: one under Savile, one under Widdrington, and one under Sir John Henderson. The force was only small, numbering under 3000, but decisive battles have often been won by small armies. The Parliamentarian army was a little larger and probably totalled little over 4000.

The course of the battle was surprising. The wings, Henderson and Savile, were level and to the fore, Widdrington in the centre was about 500 yards behind. The Parliamentarians were drawn up with one detachment behind the other, Cromwell in the lead, Fairfax in the centre and Manchester in the rear. The Roundhead intention was to block the road to Bolingbroke and cause heavy casualties to the Royalists if they tried to force a way through. As the country is open, rolling land, and the Roundhead position could easily be by-passed this did not seem the most intelligent approach, but in the event turned out to be the most effective.

However, once the first shot is fired, battle is likely to be an unpredictable matter. Henderson, on the Royalist left wing, sent his dragoons forward in a probe. Dragoons were mounted infantry whose horses had neither the physique nor the spirit for battle; thus dragoons usually dismounted and harassed the opposition with carbine and fowling-piece. If at close quarters they used swords or hand-guns – the 'dragons' (i.e. fire-breathers) from which they took their name.

As the dragoons approached Winceby farm (the Georgian

---

*The castle had belonged to the Dukes of Lancaster; it will be remembered that Henry IV was originally Henry of Bolingbroke before he took the crown from his cousin Richard II.

house), Cromwell charged. A lucky shot found his horse and while he was obtaining another the initiative passed to Fairfax, who was doubtless only too glad to vent his frustrations and settle a few scores with the Royalists. He noted that Widdrington had hung too far back, that Henderson was too far to the left, and that Savile had pushed too far forward. In a cavalry battle this was, of course, only a matter of minutes but in a fast-changing situation there is always a vital moment in which the battle may be won or lost. Often in these pages we have seen the right wing push too far ahead and drift out of the battle. This did not quite happen at Winceby, for Savile's dash to the right was too well-controlled. It is not known whether Savile intended to bypass the Roundhead position and take Manchester's division in the rear or whether he planned to converge on Cromwell's sector as that came forward to engage the dragoons. Whatever he intended was not put into effect, for just as he was streaming past the Parliamentary army on their left Fairfax put in a sudden and tremendous charge. Hit sideways with great force at a moment when they themselves seemed to possess the initiative, Savile's troops reeled to the right and back-wards. Cromwell's men soon turned to help, as did some of Manchester's although keeping a wary eye for moves from Henderson and Widdrington. But there was no trouble from them; having seen a third of the Royalist army tumbled out of their saddles, Widdrington and Henderson gave the order to retire. It was not a decision which reflected much credit on them but it may be that they saw the battle as no more than a skirmish and had no wish to sacrifice valuable men in what seemed a dubious tactic.

But it was serious enough for Savile and for Henderson's dragoons. If you turn off the A.115 towards Hammeringham you will note that the ground to the north falls away into a hollow. This is where Savile's disrupted wing soon found themselves – virtually helpless victims of the Parliamentary swordsmen, for they were trapped in a field with high hedges. To the Parliamentarians it was a lovely day, and the area is still known as 'Slash Hollow'.

Winceby was a small, strange, but important battle. It enhanced Cromwell's reputation, but Fairfax was really the architect of victory; it showed the Royalists that the opposition cavalry were as good, if not better, than their own, and should not be under-rated; and it contributed in no small measure to the ultimate Parliamentary victory.

For the visitor it has certain advantages. Although not easy to find, it is easy to look over as a whole. And, with the benefit of time and hindsight, he will probably see half a dozen ways in which it could have been won – by either side.

THE BATTLE OF
NEWARK

✣

21 March 1644

In spite of the defeats at Newbury and Winceby, the Royalists had
finished the year 1643 in a stronger position than they had started
it. Charles held the West Country, west of a line running approximately through Manchester to Portsmouth; this included the
great assets of Bristol and Oxford. He also held a substantial
portion of the north, from Berwick to Hull and Carlisle to Preston
in what was very roughly a square formation. He also held Newark,
which was a strategic strongpoint. Parliament held the remainder,
though, of course, in the areas controlled by each side there were
still pockets of resistance here and there. But in effect it was a
stalemate and to gain a clearcut victory each side hoped to enlist
outside help. Naturally enough the Parliamentarians turned to the
earnest Covenanters of the north and the Royalists to the Cath-
olics of Ireland; not unexpectedly these new allies proved frequently
to be intractable and often an embarrassment.

The Scots ultimately promised to produce an army of up to
15,000 men, but the price of it was that Parliament had to swear to
reform the English Church which the Scots felt to be highly
unsatisfactory. The Scottish view of a satisfactory church was an
extreme form of Scottish Presbyterianism. The Irish arrangement
looked like being even more difficult to accommodate, for the
Irish contingents consisted of enthusiastic Romanists and rebels
who had only recently, and for this purpose, been pardoned for
fighting against their English overlords.

Both sets of reinforcements started to arrive in England in late

1643 and early 1644. Brisk fighting began almost at once. The Hull Parliamentarians, who had been trapped in Hull for months, now emerged and cut across the country to engage the Irish army at Nantwich. By now the Marquis of Newcastle, far from putting pressure on the Parliamentarians in Hull, had himself had to fall back to York, where he was threatened by Scots from the north and Yorkshire Parliamentarians from the south.

These moves made Newark more important than ever. It had been in Royalist hands since July 1642 although in February 1643 the Roundheads had made a strong attack on it. By the spring of 1644 its strategic value was paramount. At Newark the Fosse Way (the A.46) which links Leicester, Nottingham, and Lincoln, crosses the Great North road (A.1), and all this at the point where the A.1 crosses the Trent. No one who visits this delightful town – which has a number of relics of the Civil War – can fail to grasp its strategic importance. In the Civil War that importance was that it blocked the route between the Parliamentary forces at Lincoln and those at Nottingham, Derby, and Leicester, while at the same time keeping open communications between Newcastle, York, and Oxford. As the Royalist army depended heavily on arms bought in Holland and landed at Newcastle or in Yorkshire ports, the value of the through route to Oxford was more than important: it was vital.

This being so, the Parliamentarians were determined to take it. On 29 February 1644 Sir John Meldrum moved to Newark with 7000 men. His army was composed of 2000 horse and 5000 foot. It had eleven guns and two mortars. 'Foot' were usually made up into regiments about 1200 strong of which 400 would be pikemen and the rest musketeers. The latter had early flintlocks which had a range of up to 400 yards but were far from accurate. However, accuracy was of no great account if the opposition were good enough to remain in close formation. Muskets were heavy, and were usually propped upon forked sticks; they were also slow and a rate of five rounds in ten minutes would be the best which could be expected. Within half an hour a musketeer would have discharged all the shot he could carry and would have to return or get to work

with the sword he carried. The idea of having a sword attached to
the barrel – i.e. a bayonet – had not been invented at the time of
the Civil War and if a man's sword was not in the way of his
musket, his musket would hamper him from using his sword. When
their ammunition was gone, musketeers usually retired rapidly
inside the squares formed by pikemen. The forked stick, carried for
propping up the musket when taking aim, was also useful for
putting down in front of a defensive position to discourage charging
horsemen.

The pikemen also carried swords, but with 16 to 18-foot pikes
and some body armour were slow-moving. At Pinkie, dragoons
had galloped up to pikemen, discharged their guns into their faces,
and ridden away unhurt.* But if muskets were slow, cannon were
even slower. Those at Newark seem to have had a calibre of 8 in.
and would launch a shot of about 40 lb.

On 6 March Meldrum captured Muskham bridge, over the
Trent, destroying Holles' regiment in the process. From there he
gained control of 'The Island', that part of Newark which is
enclosed by the waters of the Trent. When the reader visits Newark
he will notice various earthworks and defences but most of these
date from a later stage in the siege, and were not in existence at the
time of the battle we are describing here. Meldrum was now able
to surround Newark completely.

It was obvious that the Royalists were in a critical position.
Colonel Lucas, the governor of Belvoir Castle, a few miles away,
came over with a force to try to break Meldrum's lines, but he
failed, and was driven off. Fortunately for the Royalists, Charles
had already realized the impending danger and had sent an urgent
letter to Prince Rupert to give the matter his attention. Rupert left
Chester on the 12 March and marched southwards to Shrewsbury
and Bridgnorth, collecting reinforcements and war material as he
went, then came in to Lichfield. At Lichfield he linked up with
Lord Loughborough who had assembled about 2500 men at
Ashby de la Zouch. Meldrum tried to intercept Loughborough's

---

*Muskets are said to have derived their name from the word *moschetto*: a
form of hawk.

force but the men he sent to do this failed completely. By now Rupert had about 6500 men, which included some very good and experienced troops.

Meldrum, somewhat disconcerted at the rapidity of Rupert's moves, concentrated his army at the Spittal. Rupert was not merely intent on trying to relieve Newark; he was also fully determined to kill or capture most of Meldrum's army. By marching up from the south-west, Rupert planned that the Roundheads should not slip away. He left Bingham at 2 a.m., on a moonlit night, and occupied Beacon Hill, from which Meldrum had recently retreated. But the Roundheads were not going to retreat without a battle. Most of their army was at the Spittal (now a victim of the railway age) and was in two foot divisions, with cavalry screening the front. Rupert kept a very small troop (Colonel Gerard's) in reserve and sent Colonel Tillier's foot (about 500 strong) to attack the bridge of boats which was Meldrum's means of reaching 'The Island'. He then led the left wing himself and, with the right commanded by Colonel Sir Richard Crane, charged into the Parliamentarians. As the Royalists broke through, the Roundhead foot fell back to the defences on the Spittal. It was a lucky occasion for Rupert, for his full force had not yet come up. A hint of what might have happened was given when Colonel Rossiter, leading a force of Roundhead cavalry, burst through the Royalist lines and captured Colonel Gerard who had expected no such thing. But soon the rest of the Royalists came up and fanned out to surround Meldrum's force, and a detachment set off to capture the bridge of boats and cut off Muskham. Events went a little differently from expectations, for the Roundheads at the bridge of boats broke them and the Royalists took to their heels.

Rupert then decided that to save casualties he would starve out Meldrum; it seems that he had heard by devious means that Meldrum was very short of food, and that two or three days should suffice. Much to Meldrum's chagrin, his regiment of Norfolk redcoats mutinied; he then asked for terms.

Meldrum was granted an honourable surrender and allowed to march out with the 'Honours of War'. This seventeenth and

eighteenth-century convention allowed besieged garrisons, who
had fought well but whose position was hopeless, to march out on
reasonable terms. It suited both victor and vanquished as it saved
money, time, lives, and material. If, however, terms were refused,
the siege continued and no mercy at all would be shown to the
garrison if the citadel eventually fell. Meldrum was allowed to
march out with drums, swords, baggage, horses, personal belong-
ings, and colours, but had to leave his firearms behind. The
Royalists therefore acquired eleven cannon, two mortars, and
3000 muskets. One of the cannon was named 'Sweet Lips'. It had
been cast in Hull and was said to have derived its name from a
woman of easy virtue who had flourished in the town in the
previous century. It seems doubtful whether the Puritans would
have cared greatly for the name.

THE BATTLE OF
MARSTON MOOR

❦

2 July 1644

Newark, in spite of many pressures, held out till 1645, but on the 8 May in that year it surrendered by order of Charles. But, although the Battle of Newark had been a bright spot in Royalist fortunes in early 1643, events were not going so well for them elsewhere. The Scots were gradually moving southwards and in April linked up with Fairfax's army at Selby. The combined force was now so large and formidable that Newcastle sent an urgent message to Charles at Oxford saying that if he did not have immediate help he would soon lose the whole of the north. Charles was hard pressed to know what to do as he was short of troops himself but handed over a substantial cavalry force to Prince Rupert and told him to head north, collecting all the reinforcements he could *en route*.

Rupert left Shrewsbury on 16 May with 2000 horse and 6000 foot. He moved into Lancashire first. That county had sent so many soldiers to the Royalist armies in previous years that it had subsequently fallen to the Parliamentarians for little effort. Now, as Rupert showed the flag again, it came back to the Royalists with equal ease. He also made a few gains from elsewhere, such as Derbyshire, which supplied 500. Brig. Peter Young, who has made a lifelong study of the Civil War, considers that this probably brought Rupert's numbers up to 13,000. With this he hoped to link up with the 5000 under Newcastle in York; but first he had to break through twice his own numbers of opposing Roundheads. There was little in his favour but he himself was a man of much enterprise and dash, whereas his opponents were commanded by elderly, though experienced, generals. Perhaps his greatest asset was that the Parliamentarian force had three commanders, each of whom had firm, though unenterprising, views; they were Major-General Leslie, Lord Fairfax (father of Sir Thomas Fairfax), and the Earl of Manchester.

Rupert reached Skipton on 26 June 1644. He was then forty-three miles from York. He stayed at Skipton three days, preparing his army for the forthcoming battle.

His arrival at Skipton and his preparations were not unknown to the Roundheads. They were in somewhat of a quandary what to do. If they stayed besieging York they would be cut apart by Rupert's army. If, on the other hand, they maintained the siege of York but detached an army to deal with Rupert they would probably have been outflanked and defeated with ignominy. They therefore took the third course, which was to break off the siege and put their whole force against Rupert on his way to relieve the town. As Rupert advanced, and came to Knaresborough, a mere eighteen miles from York, they lifted the siege and deployed their combined forces, 27,000 strong. The site they chose was Marston Moor, six miles to the west of York.

This was a thoroughly sound move, and as they waited for the forthcoming battle with an army which would outnumber Rupert's by more than two to one they felt no slight confidence in the manoeuvre. But, as the hours slipped by, and nothing more than Rupert's vanguard was observed their confidence began to be displaced by irritation and finally by dismay.

Rupert, of course, was too old a hand at the game to fight where his opponents wanted him to fight, and on their terms. Furthermore he had made an accurate estimate of the strength and weaknesses of both sides. He himself had speed and manoeuvre-ability, enterprise, and a unified command. The Parliamentarians had superior numbers, little enterprise, and a triumvirate at their head. Doubtless he smiled grimly to himself as he left his advance party within sight of the Roundhead armies while he himself pressed north to Boroughbridge, where he crossed the Ure, followed it by crossing the Swale at Thornton Bridge, and came along the Ouse to York. There he relieved the town and joined up with Newcastle's men, thus gaining another 5000 men. He made it all look very easy, though if the modern visitor follows his route today he may not think it too easy, and will be somewhat impressed by the audacity of the plan.

Unfortunately for the Royalist cause, Rupert had rather more courage and dash than common sense. If he had continued to manoeuvre as skilfully as before he could have led the Round-heads a merry dance and kept a grip upon the communications of the north. But, as had been seen as early as Edgehill, once Rupert started moving he could not easily stop. Some of his troops had different ideas, and settled down to a little drinking and looting. When therefore he decided to use his increased numbers for battle, still short by some 9000 of the strength of the opposition, the Roundhead generals were astonished to hear of this turn of events. Their view, not surprisingly, had been that Rupert would now hold York and use it for a base to cut off their own communi-cations. Strategically Rupert was now in an excellent position, as his opponents knew. In fact the only move available to them seemed to be to cut off Rupert from his sources of supply. They therefore set off south-west and were approaching Tadcaster before they heard the almost incredible news that Rupert was now coming out to fight against their superior numbers. They promptly made an 'about turn' and set off back to Marston Moor. The last time they had drawn themselves up on this battlefield they were expecting an attack from the south-west; now, however, they faced one from the north-east.

Marston Moor probably looks much the same today as it did in 1644. It is an open windy plain which extends between Tock-with to the west and Long Marston to the east. The distance between the two is 1½ miles, and as the two armies deployed they covered that area evenly. The visitor will probably approach it along the B.1224 from York and turn along the Marston Lane which will take him to Tockwith. He will see a memorial on the right of this road and will note a ditch to the east of it. There is another ditch running parallel with the Marston Lane, but he may not notice this from the road. On such hazards battles are lost and won. As he moves along this road he will be passing behind the Roundhead position, with Fairfax on the right wing, Leven and Crawford in the centre, Manchester in the left centre, and Cromwell on the left wing. On the hill behind him is a knob of ground which was once covered with trees. It is known as Cromwell's Plump, and was Leven's headquarters. The ground slopes very gently towards the Royalists position and thereafter is flat. Nobody recorded how wide the ditch was at the time of the battle nor how much water it contained. On the Royalist side, Byron commanded the right wing, facing Cromwell; Eythin and Newcastle were in the centre; and Goring commanded the left, opposite the elder Fairfax; Rupert commanded the reserve. It was an ideal area for a cavalry battle – or seemed to be. Both sides were anxious for a solution by battle and both equally unaware of the urgency felt by the other side. Yet in spite of it all, the early hours of 2 July were spent by both in trying to manoeuvre their forces into the most favourable position. Had Rupert launched an attack on the Roundheads as they were coming up to the battlefield, history might have been different. Equally, if the Roundheads had launched an attack before the Royalists expected them, the battle might have had a different ending. But both sets of commanders had troubles enough of their own at that stage without thinking of giving any to the enemy. The Scots' foot had made excellent headway on the march south-west the previous day and were approaching Tadcaster before the message to return reached them. When the armies formed up at Marston Moor therefore the Roundheads were still short of some of their best infantry. But, fortunately for them, Rupert had his own troubles. When the Roundheads had left their siege-lines and come out to deploy at Marston Moor on the earlier occasion, they had abandoned all sorts of equipment which the Royalists could not forbear to loot. Then, when the Royalists were assembled, they refused to march until they received their arrears of pay. Even with all these disadvantages, Rupert would probably have been wise to attack, as his opponents were in a worse state of confusion than his own side was.

Rupert placed a line of musketeers along the ditch dividing the two armies. His own area was open moorland, superb country for cavalry manoeuvre; the Parliamentarians on the other hand had some rye fields in their territory. The Royalist musketeers were doubtless positioned to disrupt the enemy formation rather than form part of a defensive line. If the Roundheads once got themselves into a tangle, Rupert would know very well how to exploit it.

The Royalist dispositions – as would be expected – consisted of horse on the wings and foot in the centre. The right wing had about 2500 horse, the left about 2000, and the centre consisted of 10,000 foot. There were a few hundred musketeers and sixteen guns. Rupert's reserve division consisted of 650 horse. The Roundheads had, of course, the advantage of superior numbers, and this apparently gave them approximately 7000 cavalry and 20,000 foot. They had twenty-five guns.

Marston Moor was an extraordinary battle. As the day wore on, and both sides had placed their troops in what seemed to be reasonably satisfactory positions, the Roundheads waited for the inevitable Royalist attack. To their surprise it did not come. Hour succeeded hour. Apparently Rupert was having some acrimonious discussion with at least one of his subordinate commanders, but this was not the only reason for the delay. It is one thing to hurl yourself into a battle when and where you can see an obvious opportunity but an entirely different matter if the opposition outnumbers you and presents no obvious weakness. By four o'clock in the afternoon the Roundheads realized that by numbers alone the initiative probably lay with them. However, they did not act at once; instead they waited till evening when they could see from their slight eminence that the Royalists had dismounted, had lighted fires, and were taking an evening meal. It seemed too good an opportunity to miss. At a single cannon shot the whole Roundhead army moved forward. Darkness seemed to have fallen early for August and now the reason was seen. There was a clap of thunder and a scud of rain. Marston Moor had begun with a thunderstorm.

The Royalists were surprised, and the Roundheads were over the ditch before Rupert's force had alerted sufficiently to check them. On the right, Sir Thomas Fairfax pushed well ahead and routed the extreme left of Goring's wing. Making the perennial mistake he set off in pursuit but by the time he had broken off and rallied his troop he found that the rest of Goring's men had spotted the gap and with a desperate charge cut up the Roundheads very badly. Fairfax, seeing the hopeless disarray of his command, promptly retired from the field.

But it was harder going in the Roundhead centre. As the Royalists set to with their normal dash, the Scottish troops reeled and staggered under the blow. But they held. Then up came the Scottish second line, and it was the turn of the Royalists to fall back. So far, the Roundhead right had been beaten and the centre was just holding its own. On the left, however, it was a very different story.

Cromwell, who commanded the Roundhead left wing consisting of 3000 men, had hurtled into Byron's troops. Byron – his opposite – had apparently made a tactical mistake in that instead of letting his musketeers disrupt the Roundhead formation and then widen the gaps, he had charged himself and made it impossible to use his musketeers. As a result, although the Royalists checked the Roundhead charge with much difficulty, their losses were very heavy and the Roundheads were soon in control. The only bright spot for the Royalists was that Cromwell himself was wounded; unfortunately for the Royalists it was not serious and soon 'Old Noll' was back in command.

Rupert, seeing that disaster was opening up on this wing, now flung himself and his reserve into the fray. It was in vain. Although the vigour and desperation of his charge, combined with some very pretty swordwork, enabled him to break through the Roundhead lines, he was soon surrounded by Scottish foot. This is when he desperately needed more Royalist foot, or better still another wing of cavalry. But he had nothing to match the dour Scottish infantry, commanded by Leslie, and soon was in flight himself.

Yet, although the battle was now virtually won for the Parliamentarians, the confusion on the field was so great that few of the combatants had any idea of the position.

On both sides terrified men were fleeing from the field. Royalists on the right were rushing for safety over Tockwith Moor, while in the Roundhead centre many of the Scottish foot were wishing they had never left Scotland, which they certainly never expected to see again. Some of the commanders were in similar confusion.

At this delicate stage, with a Parliamentarian victory virtually won but with an excellent chance of its being frittered away in the general confusion, leaving a stalemate, Fairfax, who had lost his command, came over to the Roundhead left. There he met Cromwell, whose wound had been tended, and who was now looking for a decisive part to play. This was the 'luck of battle' – the opportunity which is presented to some commanders but never to others. Fairfax reported his own success which had turned to failure, and Cromwell was able to make an assessment of the general scene. The situation in the middle was stable enough and favouring the Roundheads; the Roundhead right wing was in confusion with the Royalists now plundering Fairfax's baggage-wagons; but the Roundhead left had complete victory and capacity to spare. It was the work of minutes for Cromwell to assemble a cavalry force and turn it on to the Royalist left wing. By moving forward and then wheeling sharply right Cromwell was able to come on to the rear of Goring's men. There are few situations more disconcerting than to be attacked in the rear at the time when you think you are consolidating an undisputed victory. Goring's division was no exception; surprise and confusion at this unexpected attack from an impossible source filled them with confusion and dismay; they put up little fight. The last to give up the struggle were Newcastle's Whitecoats. Here there was no dismay, no panic. Surrounded, and without hope of assistance they fought on, scorning surrender. The casualties in this battle were high, and particularly so in this quarter of the field. The Royalists were said to have lost over 4000 killed; 1500 were taken prisoner. The Roundheads got off much more lightly, losing a mere 300 killed, although many more had sword cuts to remember the battle by. But, as we have often seen in these pages, the heaviest casualties may occur when the battle is virtually over, sometimes completely over, and naturally enough, to the losing side. Nevertheless, the huge disparity between the casualty figures on each side requires some explanation. How did 4000 men meet their deaths for a cost of only 300?

Clearly a good number, possibly a hundred or two, fell in the first charge made by Fairfax from the right wing of the Parliamentarian army. We recall Fairfax's cavalry doing terrible execution at Winceby in 'Slash Hollow' the previous October. Doubtless they were equally effective among the bushes and clumps running across the moor. There would have been other heavy casualties on this (the left of the Royalist army) when Cromwell put in that final charge into the rear of Goring's men who were caught plundering. Many had probably discarded their weapons and were staggering along with armsful of loot, under the impression that the battle was won and it was a Royalist victory.

Equally there would have been a number of casualties in the other wing. Many would have fallen on both sides – in Cromwell's first charge. It will be recalled that Cromwell launched 3000 men, and 3000 men can cause a lot of damage. After Cromwell had left the field, his men – now commanded by the dashing Major-General Lawrence Crawford – sustained a series of heavy charges by Rupert's force. Rupert, of course, was well aware that victory or defeat hung in the balance in this quarter, and spared no effort. Rupert, as we saw, cut and slashed his way through, but was then engulfed by the Scots foot under Leslie. It seems that Rupert was unhorsed, for it was reported that he had to hide himself in a beanfield. Presumably, darkness had now fallen.

The credit for final victory probably lay with Fairfax, who seems to have wandered about the field, even through the Royalist lines, unrecognised. When he met Cromwell that portion of the battlefield must have looked something like his own earlier, though doubtless more bloody. Experience told him that this was a point in which half the Roundhead army could easily disappear from the field in pursuit – or perhaps under the impression that they had lost the battle if they were near enough to see what was happening to the remnants of their right wing, now being plundered by the Royalists under Goring.

Even so, these desperate killing-grounds would only seem to account for about half the Royalist casualties. Where then did the others come from?

It is not possible to be sure but it would seem that they would mainly be musketeers, who were handled very ineptly in this battle. Apart from those lining the ditch, who were ridden over in the first charge, there were three regiments of musketeers, each numbering about 750, who were positioned ahead of the Royalist army, covering the centre. Doubtless they were meant to disrupt the Roundhead advance and perhaps fire into the flanks of cavalry as they swept by. Possibly they were not meant to remain in that position at all, but the surprise of the Roundhead advance caught them unawares. They were – to use a military cynicism – candidates for 'six feet of earth or a decoration'. As it was, they undoubtedly got the six feet of earth. It seems likely that they would have been wiped out almost to a man, just like the Whitecoats (they were in fact drawn from Rupert's Bluecoats, and Byron's regiment). But had the battle gone the other way they would have been the heroes of a Royalist victory.

As we have seen, Marston Moor was a decisive battle, and went to the Roundheads partly because of their initiative and partly because of Royalist mistakes. It was, of course, somewhat foolhardy of Rupert to take on superior numbers when his own men were exhausted by the strenuous manoeuvres of the previous few days. But decisive or not, the Roundheads made singularly poor use of their victory. Not only had they destroyed an army; they had also badly damaged Prince Rupert's reputation. He was no longer the invincible cavalry commander. In that process Cromwell's own reputation had increased even further. Cromwell had the modern approach of careful and ruthless selection of his subordinate commanders. There was one criterion – and it was merit.

Rupert's reputation was not the only one to be damaged in this battle, and the criticism of him was as a battle commander rather than on personal grounds. The same cannot be said of some of the other commanders. Eythin had criticized Rupert's battle-plan and probably contributed to the delay which eventually induced the Roundheads to attack. Newcastle was over-cautious and Goring – though the most successful Royalist commander – perhaps too reckless. On the Parliamentarian side Lord Fairfax, father of the dashing cavalry commander, Sir Thomas Fairfax, was so dispirited at seeing his infantry routed that he rode off the battlefield, went to his home ten miles away and straight to bed. Leven and Manchester both rode off the field but, whereas Manchester subsequently collected both his wits and some fugitives and returned, Leven was well up with the leaders in his panic flight and did not stop – it is said – till he reached Leeds. There must have been some ingenious explanations when some of these distinguished generals were subsequently required to comment on their actions. They had plenty of time to do so, for the Roundheads camped at Marston Moor for two days, trying to reorganize, and hardly aware that they had won a battle. Rupert was a little quicker to recover. He assembled the remnants of his cavalry in York and eventually collected some 10,000 men to march north-west, to meet Montrose. He was in no danger of pursuit. Having given thanks to God for their great and surprising victory, the Parliamentarians saw no further ahead than retaking York. Had they pressed on towards Oxford they might have defeated Charles's 'Oxford' army, and brought the war to an end that year. But their chances were frittered away.

This was the biggest battle of the Civil War and was second only to Towton as the biggest battle ever fought on English soil. It is interesting to move from one battlefield to the other and to sense the peculiar difference and atmosphere of each. Marston Moor, of course, had many less casualties, and was less horrific, but even the pious psalm-singing Roundheads showed little mercy once their blood was stirred. Doubtless they saw themselves as inflicting due punishment on the enemies of God. Although allegedly despising the lace, the rich clothing, and the elaborate swords of the Royalists, they stripped the corpses very thoroughly; within twenty-four hours every corpse on any battlefield was stark naked, divested by the victors or by the vulture-like ghouls who trailed behind the armies to rob the dead or the defenceless. The Royalists, for their part, would feel equal justification in their victories for withholding quarter; they saw the Parliamentarians not as pioneers of democratic government but as rebels against a king appointed by divine right, and as such deserving no mercy.

THE BATTLE OF
ROWTON HEATH

24 September 1645

York surrendered to Parliament on 16 July 1644, two weeks
exactly after Marston Moor. But, even with the north virtually
gone, there was still some prospect of a Royalist victory. The
Marquis of Newcastle, admittedly, could not see it, and sailed
for Holland, taking no further part in the war, but Rupert, looking
back, considered his men had acquitted themselves reasonably
well against superior numbers. However, prospects looked bleak
in the south midlands where Parliament had two considerable
armies, commanded by the Earl of Essex and Sir William Waller.
Fortunately for the Royalists both these commanders had a high
opinion of their own abilities and a low opinion of the other's.
That fact, often expressed, completely ruled out any co-operation
between them. It was a godsend for the Royalists, for they were
able to tackle each army in turn, and achieve victories. Had
Essex and Waller combined nothing could have saved the king.
Instead Charles was able to beat Waller at Cropredy Bridge in
Oxfordshire, and then turn on Essex. Essex had noted that the
export of Cornish tin paid for the import of Royalist ammunition
and therefore decided to occupy Cornwall and stop this vital
trade. He was already in Devon, where he was campaigning with
moderate success. Yet although he did not realize it at the time,
disaster was stalking him; for Charles had already decided to
bring him to battle. Essex hoped that Waller would have inter-
fered with the progress of the Royal army but this proved a false
hope, and Charles was already in Launceston when Essex had

only reached Bodmin. Essex's ineptitude as a strategist was soon fully revealed, and on 2 September 1644 his hungry and bewildered army was forced to capitulate at Lostwithiel, on the River Fowey. Six thousand surrendered, and handed over forty-two guns and a mortar, and 5000 muskets. Had Charles then pursued a bold policy, he could have marched on London and probably taken it. But the general apathy which appeared to infect both sides in this war now seemed to influence him as well. Instead, he made a half-hearted attempt to capture Plymouth, which failed, and then decided to relieve besieged garrisons of Royalists in Basing House, near Basingstoke, at Donnington Castle, near Newbury, and at Banbury. Nevertheless, he dallied too long and when, in October, he decided to return to Oxford there were 18,000 Parliamentarians between him and his home base. His own force numbered approximately 9000. Notwithstanding this disadvantage, he decided to give battle at Newbury on 28 October 1644. This time the chosen site was on the north of the town, around Donnington Castle. Cromwell was not his usual enterprising self in this battle and the result was a Roundhead failure more than a Royalist victory. Charles was able to push his army through to Oxford; and later both Donnington Castle and Basing House were relieved. The war then petered out for the year 1644, and the armies went into winter quarters. (Campaigning in the winter was regarded as futile by both sides; the obvious disadvantages outweighed any chance advantages.)

However, during the lull in hostilities, two events took place which eventually led to victory for the Parliamentarians. A new regular army of 20,000 men, the 'New Model' Army, was created. At the same time, by the 'Self-denying Ordinance', command of this army was left to professional soldiers, and such well-known, though inactive, figures as Manchester and Essex retired. Into their place went vigorous professionals with Sir Thomas Fairfax at the head and Cromwell as second in command. This was the army which won the Battle of Naseby in Northamptonshire on 14 June 1645, the battle which virtually clinched the war for the Parliamentarians. Charles was not captured, and he spent the

following eight months trying to raise another army. His only
hope lay in Scotland where the Marquis of Montrose had raised
a considerable following. By 15 August Montrose had taken
Glasgow and controlled all the vital ports of Scotland. Alas for
hopes; many of Montrose's Highlanders slipped away to stow
their plunder, and, while Montrose's force was thus depleted
and small, Leslie defeated him at Philiphaugh, near Selkirk, with
the army which had been serving in England (13 September 1645).
After this victory the Covenanters took cold and savage revenge
for the slaughter of Kilsythe, when Montrose's troops had ignored
all pleas for restraint, even those issued by Montrose himself.
Leslie's dragoons now shot down prisoners in cold blood, and are
reported to have flung eighty men, women, and children off
Linlithgow Bridge into the waters of the Avon some fifty feet below.
In this tide of blood and revenge Charles's hopes for help from
Scotland now disappeared.

But the war was not quite over. Although Goring had been
defeated at Langport on 10 July and Rupert had surrendered at
Bristol on 11 September, all Charles could think of was the
brilliant campaign of Montrose in Scotland. He could scarcely
realize that all hope from that quarter would disappear for ever
within a few days. Charles deserved both admiration and criticism
at this stage. He refused to give up hope; but when Rupert surrendered Bristol, which he and others were confident he could
hold for at least four months, he turned against his nephew and
forgot the long record of devoted service and brilliant victories
Rupert had brought him. In that black autumn the Royalist
cause was crumbling everywhere, but Charles, who had not heard
the bleak news of Philiphaugh, was still optimistic in mid-Sep-
tember. Possibly he realized that his enemies were almost as bitter
between themselves as they were against him. At all events he
was holding grimly on to a small army consisting of some 3000
cavalry and 1000 infantry. He decided his best course was to
relieve Chester, which had been besieged since July, and to make
it his headquarters in the north-west. Then he would march up
through Lancashire and Cumberland, link up with Montrose,

and come back on a path of conquest, driving all before him.

Chester was besieged on the east side only; it was open on the west, where the river Dee flows. It was not therefore impossible— though it was arduous – to march around to the west side and enter the city.

However, the Parliamentarians were not to be caught napping. Their commander in that area was Colonel-General Poyntz, a dour, determined, and experienced soldier. Poyntz had tried and failed to intercept and engage Charles at Worcester but had followed in hot pursuit, even marching through the night. In consequence he arrived on the outskirts of Chester at 6 a.m. on the 24th. Poyntz knew very well that although Charles himself was in Chester with his infantry, and a few cavalry – a total of not more than 1000 – the remainder of the Royalist cavalry under Langdale was on the outside. Poyntz was short of troops himself, having not more than 3000. Langdale, with the Royalist cavalry, halted at Rowton Heath.

The situation was now nicely balanced. If Poyntz could get to the besiegers and reinforce them, there was little chance that they would be dispersed by the Royalist army. But he had no reason for great confidence, for when Langdale charged at 9 a.m. Poyntz's troops fell back in confusion. Well they might, perhaps, considering the arduous march they had just accomplished. Both sides were in desperate need of reinforcements, but Poyntz was the one lucky – or skilful – enough to get his message through. In consequence he received another 500 cavalry and 300 foot from the siege-lines. They could be of no value to the siege at this point but they could be invaluable in an open battle. There was slight risk that Langdale could turn and destroy the remainder of the besiegers, for their lines were totally unsuitable for any cavalry action.

By the time Charles realized the situation, and appreciated the need to send out help to Langdale, Poyntz had attacked. It was then 3 p.m. The Royalist reinforcements were too late to influence the battle but not too late to be killed in it. Langdale's men attacked by Poyntz in the front, and harassed by the foot soldiers under Colonel Jones, were driven right back to the walls of Chester. There they fell into an appalling tangle with the rest of the Roundhead besiegers, as well as the reinforcements recently sent out from the city of Chester. Those inside the city manned the walls (which the visitor will doubtless walk around) and fired into the struggling mass at what they hoped were the right targets. Gradually the Roundheads gained the upper hand and forced the Royalists away from the walls in the direction of Hoole Heath. The Royalist cavalry, who found themselves battling in narrow and congested streets, had already tasted defeat at Marston Moor and Naseby and their morale was brittle. Six hundred were killed and 800 taken prisoner. Thus ended Charles' hopes of linking up with Montrose, of whose defeat he was still ignorant.

It is still possible to follow the course of this battle today by crossing the Dee at Holt Bridge and proceeding, like Langdale's cavalry, to Rowton Heath. The visitor will find the site of the first attack at Hatton Moor, on the A.41 to Whitchurch and should then go on to Rowton Heath. He will find an inn – of later date – called 'Ye Old Trooper', then perhaps enter the city and look over the battlefield from the walls. Standing up there he will not be surprised to think that Chester still held out till 3 February 1646.

THE BATTLE OF PRESTON

🦂

17 August 1648

The final stages of the first phase of the Civil War dragged on till 19 August 1646, although Charles himself had surrendered to the Scots on 5 May 1646. They were besieging Newark at the time and Charles felt he would fare better politically in their hands than with the English Parliamentarians. Oxford, however, was not surrendered till 24 June, and the Marquis of Worcester defied the Roundheads at Raglan Castle until 19 August.

The Scots were delighted to be host to Charles and promised to assist his restoration to the throne, provided he would make Presbyterianism the religion of England. Much as Charles wished for the throne this condition was too great a burden for his will and his conscience. It would, he felt, be selling his soul, for he was by conscience, a High Churchman. After a time, the Scots wearied of his apparent dallying and handed him over to the English Parliament. This is no place to describe the shades of religious opinion which functioned in the English Parliament, but it may be noted that the intensity with which beliefs were held made agreement or compromise almost impossible. Charles observed, and waited. The Presbyterians were in the majority in Parliament but a minority in the nation. Charles therefore appeared to give careful consideration to their views, which he discussed in infinite and totally unnecessary detail, but all the while was in correspondence with a variety of possible allies, in Scotland, in France, and even in England.

In March 1647, the Presbyterians caused a crisis by issuing an order for the disbandment of the New Model Army, ostensibly because of the expense of keeping it up, but actually because it included too many of their opponents, who tended to be more tolerant though not necessarily less devout. The New Model Army, however, refused to be disbanded and with the approval of Fairfax and Cromwell removed the king from Holmby House, Northamptonshire, where he was under house arrest, and bore him off to Newmarket, the army's headquarters. The army then marched on Parliament, and as many of the Presbyterians had hastily, though perhaps prudently, removed themselves, had no difficulty about obtaining a majority. With this they offered Charles favourable terms which he would have done very well to accept.

Charles, however, leapt to the mistaken conclusion that he could do better. Seeing the conflict between the Presbyterians and the army, he came to the opinion that he could now turn the tables militarily. On 11 November 1647 he slipped away from his loose guard and reached the Isle of Wight. There he was confined to Carisbrooke Castle but not otherwise impeded. He began rapidly to organize his military return.

The effects were not seen until 28 April 1648, but on that date some north-country Royalists seized Berwick, and proclaimed for the King. Soon, there was support elsewhere. There was a rebellion in South Wales, where the army had so much resented the order to disband that it had joined with the local Royalists in Pembrokeshire. Cromwell was sent against them and was kept besieging Pembroke Castle until July. The Irish, under Lord Inchiquin, were also up in arms. The Scots voted to raise a new army, which they hoped would number nearly 40,000. Even the south-east showed Royalist sympathies. The rising in Kent was quickly suppressed by Fairfax but the trouble in the eastern counties took longer to crush. Even so, the revolt was by no means over. There were plenty more Royalist sympathizers there and elsewhere, as, for example, in the Midlands.

In Scotland the situation was not quite as promising as it looked. The Duke of Hamilton and his supporters paid lip-service to the Covenanter's ideals but their hearts were not in their cause in the same way as the Earl of Argyll. Hamilton was not a very experienced soldier and badly needed an efficient second-in-command. In the event, he received the Earl of Callander, an ardent Royalist, and an authoritarian of rigid political and military views.

Although by no means ready for a trial of strength, Hamilton invaded England on 9 July with a mixed force, many of whom had no proper training, let alone battle experience. His force was short of every necessary supply, including ammunition. It had to try to live on the country it passed through and, as the weather was unbelievably adverse, with bitter winds and driving incessant rain, the condition of this army may be imagined.

Hamilton rested for six days at Carlisle, where he was reinforced by Langdale who brought 3000 foot and some cavalry. Lambert, his Parliamentarian opponent, had not the numbers to match him, and fell back to Penrith. Hamilton followed up quickly, though not perhaps quickly enough, but was unable to trap Lambert in Appleby, where they had a brief clash. Lambert disengaged and Hamilton paused in the area, waiting for reinforcements which trickled in very slowly and inadequately. All this was taking far too long, for in July Cromwell was free of Pembrokeshire and able to head north. But even his army was in a poor state, ill-shod, and much battered by the weather which made the going so bad. Every day that passed, however, made Hamilton's men less welcome in the north; they behaved like a conquering army intent on sacking their newly-acquired territory.

On 2 August Hamilton reached Kendal, and remained there for a week. Meanwhile Lambert withdrew, first to Richmond, then to Ripon and then to Knaresborough. These were good tactics, for he blocked the way to Yorkshire, and steered Hamilton toward Lancashire, while all the time threatening his flank. Hamilton was desperately short of food, guns, ammunition, and transport. However, he was joined by about 3000 Scottish reinforcements from Ulster, commanded by Sir George Monro. Almost immediately conflict broke out between Monro and Callander, for Monro would not take orders from Callander and Callander would not tolerate Monro as part of his army unless under command. The solution was to send Monro's invaluable reinforcements to Kirkby Lonsdale, where they were supposed to wait for promised supplies and ordnance from Scotland. Hamilton then moved on to Hornby and paused for another five days.

At this point Hamilton's men held council of war and decided on policy without having any idea where Lambert and Cromwell were. They debated whether to proceed through Yorkshire or Lancashire, London being the objective. In the end Lancashire was chosen, and they set off south completely ignorant of the fact that Cromwell was now at Otley and was heading for Skipton where he would cross the Pennines. Hamilton's army was very strung out, and extended over sixteen miles; this was because he did not want to put too much pressure on local resources when they halted, though the decision can hardly have been made on grounds of clemency.

Cromwell, who knew the country well, and in that respect differed from Hamilton, debated when and where to hit the Scots. He was heavily outnumbered, having only 8000 to pit against nearly 18,000, with another 4000 following up. However, he knew exactly what he was doing, which was more than could be said for his adversaries. He therefore planned to attack when Hamilton's infantry began to cross the Ribble. Langdale took the first shock, for he realized what was in Cromwell's mind and determined that the Roundheads should not prevent Hamilton's men crossing. Langdale had at least the advantage of a strong position straddling the road from Longridge to Preston. The road itself was muddy and sunken and on either side were fields surrounded by hedges and ditches. Langdale had manned all the vantage points well but it was ridiculous that such a small force as his should be opposing such a vital Roundhead thrust when not far away the Royalists had vastly superior numbers. Ahead of him lay Ribbleton Moor where he had also stationed a few outposts. Regrettably for Langdale many of his troops were raw levies and they panicked at the first drive forward by Cromwell's veterans; however, some stood firm. Soon it settled to a desperate struggle to force a path through the sunken road, with the flanks trying to clear a way along the side through the well-defended fields. Right in the thick of it was Cromwell's Lancashire regiment. Once the fighting had settled down there was no more panic among Langdale's men, outnumbered two to one though they were, and at times they were driving the Round-heads back. But, eventually, numbers told and they were pushed back into the town.

While this was going on, Hamilton was quite unaware of the critical situation which was developing fast. He himself was well back, on Preston Moor (1¼ miles north of the town), but when reports were brought to him he promptly sent forward a small party of infantry and some ammunition. His own view was that the Roundheads must be offered battle and that Preston Moor was the best place for it. It must have been somewhat disconcerting to realize that Cromwell had plans of his own and they did not include giving Hamilton a chance to defeat him. After an acrimonious council with Callander, Hamilton decided to abandon his plan to fight on Preston Moor, and press on to the town. Callander, per-haps, had too much recollection of the feats of Cromwell's cavalry to wish to be caught in the open on the Moor. Hamilton therefore sent the infantry over the bridge, leaving two brigades holding the bridge itself. This, of course, meant leaving the unfortunate Langdale force to carry on fighting as best they could, which at that stage was not very well, for some of Cromwell's men were now in Preston. Langdale himself was not with them but was back with Hamilton.

When Cromwell's vanguard entered Preston they soon turned their attention to the bridge. It was obvious that, if they once gained control, Hamilton's infantry would be massacred very quickly and expertly and the effect on his army of losing its van, being attacked on the flanks, and harassed at the rear, would soon be devastating. The battle became like a mongoose (Crom-well) attacking a sleepy snake (Hamilton). However, whatever was wrong with Hamilton's organization there was nothing wrong with his courage. Assembling a small party, which included Langdale, Hamilton led forward a forlorn hope, which involved crossing a flooded ford. At this point his personal courage – for he led the charges himself – enabled him to beat back the Roundheads while the infantry vanguard got back across the river. They then formed up near Walton Hall on the banks of the Darwen. The brigades at the bridge hung on grimly but were eventually forced off it by repeated pike charges. They fell back to rejoin the others at Walton.

Night fell, but the battle was clearly not decided. The armies mostly lay down in the mud where they had been standing. They were soaked with rain, cold, and hungry.

During that evening Hamilton held urgent councils. Callander proposed a retreat in order to link up with the rear portion and unify the force. After some dissent, this was agreed. Orders were given for the powder to be blown up by a time fuse but this was neglected, and Cromwell captured it intact. (He had already captured their baggage-wagons and Hamilton's plate.)

The Royalists set off in the night and were well on the road to Wigan by the time Cromwell realized what had happened. He did not take long to react and set off in hot pursuit. The Scots were in serious trouble in the muddy lanes, lost their way, and failed to link up as planned. But they gave a good account of themselves when attacked. On the morning of the 18th they reached Wigan and would have made a stand, but the powder they were carrying was wet and there was no more to replace it. They pressed on to Warrington, but at Winwick, where a lane and a bank made the nucleus of a defensive position, they stood. For several hours the battle raged between the half-starved, weary Scots, and Cromwell's outnumbered but jubilant Roundheads. Some of the heaviest fighting took place on the green by Winwick Church, but eventually, after a thousand Scots had fallen, the rest retreated to Warrington, where they barricaded the bridge and prepared to fight again. But the Battle of Preston was over. Hamilton and Callander set off north, after telling the remaining 2500 Scots to make the best terms they could. They did not see the campaign as lost, and were planning to link up with other Royalists elsewhere – in Wales or the Home Counties. Gradually, however, their remaining forces were thinned by desertion and sickness, and, finally, on 25 August Hamilton was taken prisoner at Stafford. Hamilton would have made an excellent company commander, brave, loyal, and persistent; but in any task requiring planning and staff work, assessment and administration, he was disastrous.

The second phase of the Civil War had ended in defeat and disgrace for the Royalists. Even worse, all trust had gone, and the Parliamentarians felt that they must punish, and take no further chances. Hamilton, Lucas, Lisle, and Holland, were all executed, and many of those who had served under them were transported to the Barbados plantations.

Nor was there any sympathy for Charles. He had twice tried to escape from Carisbrooke; now he was put under close guard at Hurst. The army had now had enough of both the Presbyterians and Charles. The former were dealt with by a military *coup d'état*, when forty-one were imprisoned and ninety-six told never to come near the House of Commons again.

On 1 January 1649 the King was put on trial on grounds that 'to levy war against the Parliament and realm of England was treason'. Charles refused to plead in any way. On 30 January 1649 he was beheaded on a scaffold erected before the windows of Whitehall Palace (now demolished). He met his death with courage and dignity.

Three Contemporary Accounts
of the Battle of Otterburn

Unlike most medieval battles, there is a wealth of contemporary information on Otterburn. Furthermore, the writers seem to be describing the same battle! All too often we find that contemporary accounts are mutually contradictory. This may have several different causes. One is that chroniclers liked to embellish the story for propaganda purposes; another is that the events were not set down till some time had elapsed; a third is that those who knew what really happened probably did not survive to tell the tale, while those who did had to invent a convincing explanation of why they themselves were not killed but had nevertheless behaved with courage and fortitude.

Froissart wrote of many battles and events and was a witness of much that he wrote about. His *Chronicles* were translated (on the orders of Henry VIII) by John Bourchier, Lord Berners (1467–1532), whose ancestors are occasionally mentioned in the French campaigns. Froissart throws much light on medieval armies, how they became lost or disorganized; how they would sometimes nearly starve to death while at other times make themselves sick with gluttony; how they could be an abject rabble and yet turn into an heroic fighting force.

The three accounts which follow provide an interesting study in medieval chronicling. It will be noticed that just as there is scarcely any perspective in medieval drawings, so there is little in medieval descriptions. But once you are familiar with the main events the contemporary descriptions come to life and convey the atmosphere of the times. We, in the twentieth century, are interested in the causes and the course of the battle; in the fourteenth and fifteenth centuries the listener or reader was principally interested in the details of the personal combat. He wanted to know where the arrow struck or how many sword-cuts it took to kill a man; in many ways he was like the modern man who reads a newspaper account of a boxing match, noting with interest and satisfaction which were the vital blows, and how and when they were delivered.

Thomas Percy, who collected together and published a number of old ballads in his *Reliques of Ancient English Poetry*, began life as a poor grocer's son and ended it as a bishop. Having had a grammar school education in Bridgnorth, Shropshire, a town rich in historical remains, he obtained an exhibition to Christ Church, Oxford, and from there went into the Church. Fortunately he had the leisure and interest to devote himself to collecting ballads which might otherwise have been lost, or worse, 'doctored' by a less scrupulous editor. The text he used places his version in the mid-fifteenth century, probably about fifty years after the battle took place.

Ballads tended to be embellished with local references, and also adapted to suit the tastes of the audience. Chevy-Chase was blended with a typical border ballad of a local challenge between the Percy family and the Douglases, and is set at a later date, though only by a few years, than Otterburn. Yet the reader will notice that the names are the same in both Froissart's prose account, 'The Ancient Ballad of Chevy-Chase', and 'The Battle of Otterbourne' which follows it. 'The Battle of Otterbourne' gives the English view of the conflict but was, in fact, written by a Scot. This was made clear in the text by such statements as that in the first verse when the writer dates the poem by saying it 'fell about the Lammas-tide/When husbands win their hay'. The hay harvest would then have been gathered in a full month by the English husbandmen.

When the English lords saw that their squire returned not again at the time appointed, and could know nothing what the Scots did, nor what they were purported to do, then they thought well that their squire was taken. The lords sent each to other, to be ready whensoever they should hear that the Scots were abroad: as for their messenger, they thought him but lost.

Now let us speak of the earl Douglas and other, for they had more to do than they that went by Carlisle. When the earls of Douglas, of Moray, of Mare departed from the great host, they took their way thinking to pass the water and to enter into the bishopric of Durham, and to ride to the town and then to return, brenning and exiling the country, and so to come to Newcastle and to lodge there in the town in the despite of all the Englishmen. And as they determined, so they did assay to put it in use, for they rode a great pace under covert without doing of any pillage by the way or assaulting of any castle, tower or house, but so came into the lord Percy's land and passed the river of Tyne without any let a three leagues above Newcastle not far from Brancepeth, and at last entered into the bishopric of Durham, where they found a good country. Then they began to make war, to slay people and to bren villages and to do many sore displeasures.

As at that time the earl of Northumberland and the other lords and knights of that country knew nothing of their coming. When tidings came to Newcastle and to Durham that the Scots were abroad, and that they might well see by the fires and smoke abroad in the country, the earl sent to Newcastle his two sons and sent commandment to every man to draw to Newcastle, saying to his sons: 'Ye shall go to Newcastle and all the country shall assemble there, and I shall tarry at Alnwick, which is a passage that they must pass by. If we may enclose them, we shall speed well.' Sir Henry Percy and sir Ralph his brother obeyed their father's commandment and came thither with them of the country. The Scots rode burning and exiling the country, that the smoke thereof came to Newcastle. The Scots came to the gates of Durham and scrimmished there; but they tarried not long but returned, as they had ordained before to do, and that they found by the way took and destroyed it. Between Durham and Newcastle is but twelve leagues English and a good country: there was no town, without it were closed, but it was brent, and they repassed the river of Tyne where they had passed before, and then came before Newcastle and there rested. All the English knights and squires of the country of York and bishopric of Durham were assembled at Newcastle, and thither came the seneschal of York, sir Ralph Lumley, sir Matthew Redman, captain of Berwick, sir Robert Ogle, sir Thomas Grey, sir Thomas Holton, sir John Felton, sir John Lilleburn, sir Thomas Abingdon, the baron of Hilton, sir John Coppledike and divers other, so that the town was so full of people that they wist not where to lodge.

When these three Scottish earls who were chief captains had made their enterprise in the bishopric of Durham and had sore overrun the country, then they returned to Newcastle and there rested and tarried two days, and every day they scrimmished. The earl of Northumberland's two sons were two young lusty knights and were ever foremost at the barriers to scrimmish. There were many proper feats of arms done and achieved: there was fighting hand to hand: among other there fought hand to hand the earl Douglas and sir Henry Percy, and by force of arms the earl Douglas won the pennon of sir Henry Percy's, wherewith he was sore displeased and so were all the Englishmen. And the earl Douglas said to sir Henry Percy: 'Sir, I shall bear this token of your prowess into Scotland and shall set it on high on my castle of Dalkeith, that it may be seen far off.' 'Sir,' quoth sir Henry, 'ye may be sure ye shall not pass the bounds of this country till ye be met withal in such wise that ye shall make none avaunt thereof.' 'Well, sir,' quoth the earl Douglas, 'come this night to my lodging and seek for your pennon: I shall set it before my lodging and see if ye will come to take it away.' So then it was late, and the Scots withdrew to their lodgings and refreshed them with such as they had. They had flesh enough: they made that night good watch, for they thought surely to be awakened for the words they had spoken, but they were not, for sir Henry Percy was counselled not so to do.

The next day the Scots dislodged and returned towards their own country, and so came to a castle and a town called Pontland, whereof sir Edmund of Alphel was lord, who was a right good knight. There the Scots rested, for they came thither betimes, and understood that the knight was in his castle. Then they ordained to assail the castle, and gave a great assault, so that by force of arms they won it and the knight within it. Then the town and castle was brent; and from thence the Scots went to the town and castle of Otterburn, an eight English mile from Newcastle and there lodged. That day they made none assault, but the next morning they blew their horns and made ready to assail the castle, which was strong, for it stood in the marish. That day they assaulted till they were weary, and did nothing. Then they sowned the retreat and returned to their lodgings. Then the lords drew to council to determine what they should do. The most part were of the accord that the next day they should dislodge without giving of any assault and to draw fair and easily towards Carlisle. But the earl Douglas brake that counsel and said: 'In despite of sir Henry Percy, who said he would come and win again his pennon, let us not depart hence for two or three days. Let us assail this castle: it is pregnable: we shall have double honour. And then let us see if he will come and fetch his pennon: he shall be well defended.' Every man accorded to his saying, what for their honour and for the love of him. Also they lodged there at their ease, for there was none that troubled them: they made many lodgings of boughs and great herbs and fortified their camp sagely with the marish that was thereby, and their carriages were set at the entry into the marishes and had all their beasts within the marish. Then they apparelled for to assault the next day: this was their intention.

Now let us speak of sir Henry Percy and of sir Ralph his brother and shew somewhat what they did. They were sore displeased that the earl Douglas had won the pennon of their arms: also it touched greatly their honours, if they did not as sir Henry Percy said he would; for he had said to the earl Douglas that he should not carry his pennon out of England, and also he had openly spoken it before all the knights and squires that were at Newcastle. The Englishmen there thought surely that the earl Douglas' band was but the Scots' vanguard and that their host was left behind. The knights of the country, such as were well expert in arms, spake against sir Henry Percy's opinion and said to him: 'Sir, there fortuneth in war oftentimes many losses. If the earl Douglas have won your pennon, he bought it dear, for he came to the gate to seek it and was well beaten: another day ye shall win as much of him or more. Sir, we say this because we know well all the power of Scotland is abroad in the fields, and if we issue out and be not men enow to fight with them, and peradventure they have made this scrimmish with us to the intent to draw us out of the town, and the number that they be of, as it is said, above forty thousand men, they may soon enclose us and do with us what they will. Yet it were better to lose a pennon than two or three hundred knights and squires and put all our country in adventure.' These words refrained sir Henry and his brother, for they would do nothing against counsel. Then tidings came to them by such as had seen the Scots and seen all their demeanour and what way they took and where they rested.

It was shewed to sir Henry Percy and to his brother and to the other knights and squires that were there, by such as had followed the Scots from Newcastle and had well advised their doing, who said to sir Henry and to sir Ralph: 'Sirs, we have followed the Scots privily and have discovered all the country. The Scots be at Pontland and have taken sir Edmund Alphel in his own castle, and from thence they be gone to Otterburn and there they lay this night. What they will do tomorrow we know not: they are ordained to abide there: and, sirs, surely their great host is not with them, for in all they pass not there a three thousand men.' When sir Henry heard that, he was joyful and said: 'Sirs, let us leap on our horses, for by the faith I owe to God and to my lord my father I will go seek for my pennon and dislodge them this same night.' Knights and squires that heard him agreed thereto and were joyous, and every man made him ready.

The same evening the bishop of Durham came thither with a good company, for he heard at Durham how the Scots were before

Newcastle and how that the lord Percy's sons with other lords and knights should fight with the Scots: therefore the bishop of Durham to come to the rescue had assembled up all the country and so was coming to Newcastle. But sir Henry Percy would not abide his coming, for he had with him six hundred spears, knights and squires, and an eight thousand footmen. They thought that sufficient number to fight with the Scots, if they were not but three hundred spears and three thousand of other. Thus they departed from Newcastle after dinner and set forth in good order, and took the same way as the Scots had gone and rode to Otterburn, a seven little leagues from thence and fair way, but they could not ride fast because of their foot-men. And when the Scots had supped and some laid down to their rest, and were weary of travailing and assaulting of the castle all that day, and thought to rise early in the morning in cool of the day to give a new assault, therewith suddenly the Englishmen came on them and entered into the lodgings, weening it had been the masters' lodgings, and therein were but varlets and servants. Then the Englishmen cried, 'Percy, Percy!' and entered into the lodgings, and ye know well where such affray of noise is soon raised: and it fortuned well for the Scots, for when they saw the Englishmen came to wake them, then the lords sent a certain of their servants of foot-men to scrimmish with the Englishmen at the entry of the lodgings, and in the mean time they armed and apparelled them, every man under his banner and under his captain's pennon. The night was far on, but the moon shone so bright as an it had been in a manner day. It was in the month of August and the weather fair and temperate.

Thus the Scots were drawn together and without any noise departed from their lodgings and went about a little mountain, which was greatly for their advantage. For all the day before they had well advised the place and said among themselves: 'If the Englishmen come on us suddenly, then we will do thus and thus, for it is a jeopardous thing in the night if men of war enter into our lodgings. If they do, then we will draw to such a place, and thereby other we shall win or lose.' When the Englishmen entered into the field, at the first they soon overcame the varlets, and as they entered further in, always they found new men to busy them and to scrimmish with them. Then suddenly came the Scots from about the mountain and set on the Englishmen or they were ware, and cried their cries; whereof the Englishmen were sore astonied. Then they cried 'Percy!' and the other party cried 'Douglas!'

There began a cruel battle and at the first encounter many were overthrown of both parties; and because the Englishmen were a great number and greatly desired to vanquish their enemies, and rested at their pace and greatly did put aback the Scots, so that the Scots were near discomfited. Then the earl James Douglas, who was young and strong and of great desire to get praise and grace, and was willing to deserve to have it, and cared for no pain nor travail, came forth with his banner and cried, 'Douglas, Douglas!' and sir Henry Percy and sir Ralph his brother, who had great indignation against the earl Douglas because he had won the pennon of their arms at the barriers before Newcastle, came to that part and cried, 'Percy!' Their two banners met and their men: there was a sore fight: the Englishmen were so strong and fought so valiantly that they reculed the Scots back. There were two valiant knights of Scots under the banner of the earl Douglas, called sir Patrick of Hepbourn and sir Patrick his son. They acquitted themselves that day valiantly: the earl's banner had been won, an they had not been: they defended it so valiantly and in the rescuing thereof did such feats of arms, that it was greatly to their recommendation and to their heirs' for ever after.

It was shewed me by such as had been at the same battle, as well by knights and squires of England, as of Scotland, at the house of the earl of Foix – for anon after this battle was done I met at Orthez two squires of England called John of Chateauneuf and John of Cantiron; also when I returned to Avignon I found also there a knight and a squire of Scotland; I knew them and they knew me by such tokens as I shewed them of their country, for I, author of this book, in my youth had ridden nigh over all the realm of Scotland, and I was as then a fifteen days in the house of earl William Douglas, father to the same earl James, of whom I spake of now, in a castle a five leagues from Edinburgh in the country of Dalkeith;

the same time I saw there this earl James, a fair young child, and a sister of his called the lady Blanche – and I was informed by both these parties how this battle was as sore a battle fought as lightly hath been heard of before of such a number; and I believe it well, for Englishmen on the one party and Scots on the other party are good men of war, for when they meet there is a hard fight without sparing, there is no ho between them as long as spears, swords, axes or daggers will endure, but lay on each upon other, and when they be well beaten and that the one party hath obtained the victory, they then glorify so in their deeds of arms and are so joyful, that such as be taken they shall be ransomed or they go out of the field, so that shortly each of them is so content with other that at their departing courteously they will say, 'God thank you': but in fighting one with another there is no play nor sparing, and this is true, and that shall well appear by this said rencounter, for it was as valiantly foughten as could be devised, as ye shall hear.

Knights and squires were of good courage on both parties to fight valiantly: cowards there had no place, but hardiness reigned with goodly feats of arms, for knights and squires were so joined together at hand strokes, that archers had no place of nother party. There the Scots shewed great hardiness and fought merrily with great desire of honour: the Englishmen were three to one: howbeit, I say not but Englishmen did nobly acquit themselves, for ever the Englishmen had rather been slain or taken in the place than to fly. Thus, as I have said, the banners of Douglas and Percy and their men were met each against other, envious who should win the honour of that journey. At the beginning the Englishmen were so strong that they reculed back their enemies: then the earl Douglas, who was of great heart and high of enterprise, seeing his men recule back, then to recover the place and to shew knightly valour he took his axe in both his hands, and entered so into the press that he made himself way in such wise, that none durst approach near him, and he was so well armed that he bare well off such strokes as he received. Thus he went forward like a hardy Hector, willing alone to conquer the field and to discomfit his enemies: but at last he was encountered with three spears all at once, the one strake him on the shoulder, the other on the breast and the stroke glinted down to his belly, and the third strake him in the thigh, and sore hurt with all three strokes, so that he was borne perforce to the earth and after that he could not be again relieved. Some of his knights and squires followed him, but not all, for it was night, and no light but by the shining of the moon. The Englishmen knew well they had borne one down to the earth, but they wist not who it was; for if they had known that it had been the earl Douglas, they had been thereof so joyful and so proud that the victory had been theirs. Nor also the Scots knew not of that adventure till the end of the battle; for if they had known it, they should have been so sore despaired and discouraged that they would have fled away. Thus as the earl Douglas was felled to the earth, he was stricken into the head with an axe, and another stroke through the thigh: the Englishmen passed forth and took no heed of him: they thought none otherwise but that they had slain a man of arms. On the other part the earl George de la March and of Dunbar fought right valiantly and gave the Englishmen much ado, and cried, 'Follow Douglas', and set on the sons of Percy: also earl John of Moray with his banner and men fought valiantly and set fiercely on the Englishmen, and gave them so much to do that they wist not to whom to attend.

Of all the battles and encounterings that I have made mention of heretobefore in all this history, great or small, this battle that I treat of now was one of the sorest and best foughten without cowardice or faint hearts. For there was nother knight nor squire but that did his devoir and fought hand to hand: this battle was like the battle of Becherel, the which was valiantly fought and endured. The earl of Northumberland's sons, sir Henry and sir Ralph Percy, who were chief sovereign captains, acquitted themselves nobly, and sir Ralph Percy entered in so far among his enemies that he was closed in and hurt, and so sore handled that his breath was so short, that he was taken prisoner by a knight of the earl of Moray's called sir John Maxwell. In the taking the Scottish knight demanded what he was, for it was in the night, so that he knew him not, and sir Ralph was so sore overcome and bled fast, that at last he said: 'I am Ralph Percy.' Then the Scot said:

'Sir Ralph, rescue or no rescue I take you for my prisoner: I am Maxwell.' 'Well,' quoth sir Ralph, 'I am content: but then take heed to me, for I am sore hurt, my hosen and my greaves are full of blood.' Then the knight saw by him the earl Moray and said: 'Sir, here I deliver to you sir Ralph Percy as prisoner; but, sir, let good heed be taken to him, for he is sore hurt.' The earl was joyful of these words and said: 'Maxwell, thou hast well won thy spurs.' Then he delivered sir Ralph Percy to certain of his men, and they stopped and wrapped his wounds: and still the battle endured, not knowing who had as then the better, for there were many taken and rescued again that came to no knowledge.

Now let us speak of the young James earl of Douglas, who did marvels in arms or he was beaten down. When he was overthrown, the press was great about him, so that he could not relieve, for with an axe he had his death's wound. His men followed him as near as they could, and there came to him sir James Lindsay his cousin and sir John and sir Walter Sinclair and other knights and squires. And by him was a gentle knight of his, who followed him all the day, and a chaplain of his, not like a priest but like a valiant man of arms, for all that night he followed the earl with a good axe in his hands and still scrimmished about the earl thereas he lay, and reculed back some of the Englishmen with great strokes that he gave. Thus he was found fighting near to his master, whereby he had great praise, and thereby the same year he was made arch-deacon of Aberdeen. This priest was called sir William of North Berwick: he was a tall man and a hardy and was sore hurt. When these knights came to the earl, they found him in an evil case and a knight of his lying by him called sir Robert Hart: he had a fifteen wounds in one place and other. Then sir John Sinclair demanded of the earl how he did. 'Right evil, cousin,' quoth the earl, 'but thanked be God there hath been but a few of mine ancestors that hath died in their beds: but, cousin, I require you think to revenge me, for I reckon myself but dead, for my heart fainteth oftentimes. My cousin Walter and you, I pray you raise up again my banner which lieth on the ground, and my squire Davie Collemine slain: but, sirs, shew nother to friend nor foe in what case ye see me in; for if mine enemies knew it, they would rejoice, and our friends discomforted.' The two brethren of Sinclair and sir James Lindsay did as the earl had desired them and raised up again his banner and cried 'Douglas!' Such as were behind and heard that cry drew together and set on their enemies valiantly and reculed back the Englishmen and many overthrown, and so drave the Englishmen back beyond the place whereas the earl lay, who was by that time dead, and so came to the earl's banner, the which sir John Sinclair held in his hands, and many good knights and squires of Scotland about him, and still company drew to the cry of 'Douglas.' Thither came the earl Moray with his banner well accompanied, and also the earl de la Mare and of Dunbar, and when they saw the Englishmen recule and their company assembled together, they renewed again the battle and gave many hard and sad strokes.

To say truth, the Englishmen were sorer travailed than the Scots, for they came the same day from Newcastle-upon-Tyne, a six English miles, and went a great pace to the intent to find the Scots, which they did: so that by their fast going they were near out of breath, and the Scots were fresh and well rested, which greatly availed them when time was of their business: for in the last scrimmish they reculed back the Englishmen in such wise, that after that they could no more assemble together, for the Scots passed through their battles. And it fortuned that sir Henry Percy and the lord of Montgomery, a valiant knight of Scotland, fought together hand to hand right valiantly without letting of any other, for every man had enough to do. So long they two fought that perforce of arms sir Henry Percy was taken prisoner by the said lord of Montgomery.

The knights and squires of Scotland, as sir Marc Adreman, sir Thomas Erskine, sir William, sir James and sir Alexander Lindsay, the lord of Fenton, sir John of Saint-Moreaulx, sir Patrick of Dunbar, sir John and sir Walter Sinclair, sir John Maxwell, sir Guy Stuart, sir John Haliburton, sir Alexander Ramsay, Robert Collemine and his two sons John and Robert, who were there made knights, and a hundred knights and squires that I cannot name, all these right valiantly did acquit themselves. And on the

English party, before that the lord Percy was taken and after, there fought valiantly sir Ralph Lumley, sir Matthew Redman, sir Thomas Ogle, sir Thomas Gray, sir Thomas Helton, sir Thomas Abingdon, sir John Lilleburn, sir William Walsingham, the baron of Helton, sir John of Colpedich, the seneschal of York and divers other footmen. Whereto should I write long process? This was a sore battle and well foughten; and as fortune is always changeable, though the Englishmen were more in number than the Scots and were right valiant men of war and well expert, and that at the first front they reculed back the Scots, yet finally the Scots obtained the place and victory, and all the foresaid Englishmen taken, and a hundred more, saving sir Matthew Redman, captain of Berwick, who when he knew no remedy nor recoverance, and saw his company fly from the Scots and yielded them on every side, then he took his horse and departed to save himself.

The same season about the end of this discomfiture there was an English squire called Thomas Waltham, a goodly and a valiant man, and that was well seen, for of all that night he would nother fly nor yet yield him. It was said he had made a vow at a feast in England, that the first time that ever he saw Englishmen and Scots in battle, he would so do his devoir to his power, in such wise that either he would be reputed for the best doer on both sides or else to die in the pain. He was called a valiant and a hardy man and did so much by his prowess, that under the banner of the earl of Moray he did such valiantness in arms, that the Scots had marvel thereof, and so was slain in fighting: the Scots would gladly have taken him alive, but he would never yield, he hoped ever to have been rescued. And with him there was a Scottish squire slain, cousin to the king of Scots, called Simon Glendowyn; his death was greatly complained of the Scots.

This battle was fierce and cruel till it came to the end of the discomfiture; but when the Scots saw the Englishmen recule and yield themselves, then the Scots were courteous and set them to their ransom, and every man said to his prisoner: 'Sirs, go and unarm you and take your ease; I am your master': and so made their prisoners as good cheer as though they had been brethren, without doing to them any damage. The chase endured a five English miles, and if the Scots had been men enow, there had none scaped, but other they had been taken or slain. And if Archambault Douglas and the earl of Fife, the earl Sutherland and other of the great company who were gone towards Carlisle had been there, by all likelihood they had taken the bishop of Durham and the town of Newcastle-upon-Tyne. I shall shew you how. The same evening that the Percies departed from Newcastle, as ye have heard before, the bishop of Durham with the rearband came to Newcastle and supped: and as he sat at the table, he had imagination in himself how he did not acquit himself well to see the Englishmen in the field and he to be within the town. Incontinent he caused the table to be taken away and commanded to saddle his horses and to sown the trumpets, and called up men in the town to arm themselves and to mount on their horses, and foot-men to order themselves to depart. And thus every man departed out of the town to the number of seven thousand, two thousand on horseback and five thousand afoot; they took their way toward Otterburn, whereas the battle had been. And by that time they had gone two mile from Newcastle tidings came to them how their men were fighting with the Scots. Therewith the bishop rested there, and incontinent came more flying fast, that they were out of breath. Then they were demanded how the matter went. They answered and said: 'Right evil; we be all discomfited: here cometh the Scots chasing of us.' These tidings troubled the Englishmen, and began to doubt. And again the third time men came flying as fast as they might. When the men of the bishopric of Durham heard of these evil tidings, they were abashed in such wise that they brake their army, so that the bishop could not hold together the number of five hundred. It was thought that if the Scots had followed them in any number, seeing that it was night, that in the entering into the town, and the Englishmen so abashed, the town had been won.

The bishop of Durham, being in the field, had good will to have succoured the Englishmen and recomforted his men as much as he could; but he saw his own men fly as well as other. Then he demanded counsel of sir William Lucy and of sir Thomas Clifford and of other knights, what was best to do. These knights for their honour would give him no counsel; for they thought to return again and do nothing should sown greatly to their blame, and to go forth might be to their great damage; and so stood still and would give none answer, and the longer they stood, the fewer they were, for some still stale away. Then the bishop said: 'Sirs, all things considered, it is none honour to put all in peril, nor to make of one evil damage twain. We hear how our company be discomfited, and we cannot remedy it: for to go to recover them, we know not with whom nor with what number we shall meet. Let us return fair and easily for this night to Newcastle, and to-morrow let us draw and go together look on our enemies.' Every man answered: 'As God will, so be it.' Therewith they returned to Newcastle. Thus a man may consider the great default that is in men that be abashed and discomfited: for if they had kept them together and have turned again such as fled, they had discomfited the Scots. This was the opinion of divers; and because they did not thus, the Scots had the victory.

I shall shew you of sir Matthew Redman, who was on horseback to save himself, for he alone could not remedy the matter. At his departing sir James Lindsay was near to him and saw how sir Matthew departed, and this sir James, to win honour, followed to chase sir Matthew Redman, and came so near him that he might have stricken him with his spear, if he had list. Then he said: 'Ah, sir knight, turn; it is a shame thus to fly: I am James of Lindsay: if ye will not turn, I shall strike you on the back with my spear.' Sir Matthew spake no word, but strake his horse with the spurs sorer than he did before. In this manner he chased him more than three miles, and at last sir Matthew Redman's horse foundered and fell under him. Then he stept forth on the earth and drew out his sword, and took courage to defend himself; and the Scot thought to have stricken him on the breast, but sir Matthew Redman swerved from the stroke, and the spear-point entered into the earth. Then sir Matthew strake asunder the spear with his sword; and when sir James Lindsay saw how he had lost his spear, he cast away the truncheon and lighted afoot, and took a little battle-axe that he carried at his back and handled it with his one hand quickly and deliverly, in the which feat Scots be well expert, and then he set at sir Matthew and defended himself properly. Thus they tourneyed together, one with an axe and the other with a sword, a long season, and no men to let them. Finally sir James Lindsay gave the knight such strokes and held him so short, that he was put out of breath in such wise that he yielded himself and said: 'Sir James Lindsay, I yield me to you.' 'Well,' quoth he, 'and I receive you, rescue or no rescue.' 'I am content,' quoth Redman, 'so ye deal with me like a good companion.' 'I shall not fail that,' quoth Lindsay, and so put up his sword. 'Well, sir,' quoth Redman, 'what will you now that I shall do? I am your prisoner, ye have conquered me. I would gladly go again to Newcastle, and within fifteen days I shall come to you into Scotland, whereas ye shall assign me.' 'I am content,' quoth Lindsay: 'ye shall promise by your faith to present yourself within this three weeks at Edinboro, and wheresoever ye go, to repute yourself my prisoner.' All this sir Matthew sware and promised to fulfil. Then each of them took their horses and took leave each of other. Sir James returned, and his intent was to go to his own company the same way that he came, and sir Matthew Redman to Newcastle.

Sir James Lindsay could not keep the right way as he came: it was dark and a mist, and he had not ridden half a mile, but he met face to face with the bishop of Durham and more than five hundred Englishmen with him. He might well escaped if he had would, but he supposed it had been his own company, that had pursued the Englishmen. When he was among them, one demanded of him what he was. 'I am,' quoth he, 'sir James Lindsay.' The bishop heard those words and stept to him and said: 'Lindsay, ye are taken: yield ye to me.' 'Who be you?' quoth Lindsay. 'I am,' quoth he, 'the bishop of Durham.' 'And from whence come you, sir?' quoth Lindsay. 'I come from the battle,' quoth the bishop, 'but I struck never a stroke there: I go back to Newcastle for this night, and ye shall go with me.' 'I may not choose,' quoth Lindsay, 'sith ye will have it so. I have taken and I am taken; such is the adventures of arms.' 'Whom have ye taken?' quoth the bishop.

'Sir,' quoth he, 'I took in the chase sir Matthew Redman.' 'And where is he?' quoth the bishop. 'By my faith, sir, he is returned to Newcastle: he desired me to trust him on his faith for three weeks, and so have I done.' 'Well,' quoth the bishop, 'let us go to Newcastle, and there ye shall speak with him.' Thus they rode to Newcastle together, and sir James Lindsay was prisoner to the bishop of Durham.

Under the banner of the earl de la Mare and of Dunbar was taken a squire of Gascoyne, called John of Chateauneuf, and under the banner of the earl of Moray was taken his companion John de Cantiron. Thus the field was clean avoided, or the day appeared. The Scots drew together and took guides and sent out scurrers to see if any men were in the way from Newcastle, to the intent that they would not be troubled in their lodgings; wherein they did wisely, for when the bishop of Durham was come again to Newcastle and in his lodging, he was sore pensive and wist not what to say nor do; for he heard say how his cousins the Percies were slain or taken, and all the knights that were with them. Then he sent for all the knights and squires that were in the town; and when they were come, he demanded of them if they should leave the matter in that case, and said: 'Sirs, we shall bear great blame if we thus return without looking on our enemies.' Then they concluded by the sun-rising every man to be armed, and on horseback and afoot to depart out of the town and to go to Otterburn to fight with the Scots. This was warned through the town by a trumpet, and every man armed them and assembled before the bridge, and by the sun-rising they departed by the gate towards Berwick and took the way towards Otterburn to the number of ten thousand, what afoot and a-horseback. They were not gone past two mile from Newcastle, when the Scots were signified that the bishop of Durham was coming to themward to fight: this they knew by their spies, such as they had set in the fields.

After that sir Matthew Redman was returned to Newcastle and had shewed to divers how he had been taken prisoner by sir James Lindsay, then it was shewed him how the bishop of Durham had taken the said sir James Lindsay and how that he was there in the town as his prisoner. As soon as the bishop was departed, sir Matthew Redman went to the bishop's lodging to see his master, and there he found him in a study, lying in a window, and said: 'What, sir James Lindsay, what make you here?' Then sir James came forth of the study to him and gave him good morrow, and said: 'By my faith, sir Matthew, fortune hath brought me hither; for as soon as I was departed from you, I met by chance the bishop of Durham, to whom I am prisoner, as ye be to me. I believe ye shall not need to come to Edinboro to me to make your finance: I think rather we shall make an exchange one for another, if the bishop be so content.' 'Well, sir,' quoth Redman, 'we shall accord right well together, ye shall dine this day with me: the bishop and our men be gone forth to fight with your men, I cannot tell what shall fall, we shall know at their return.' 'I am content to dine with you,' quoth Lindsay. Thus these two knights dined together in Newcastle.

When the knights of Scotland were informed how the bishop of Durham came on them with ten thousand men, they drew to council to see what was best for them to do, other to depart or else to abide the adventure. All things considered, they concluded to abide, for they said they could not be in a better nor a stronger place than they were in already: they had many prisoners and they could not carry them away, if they should have departed; and also they had many of their men hurt and also some of their prisoners, whom they thought they would not leave behind them. Thus they drew together and ordered so their field, that there was no entry but one way, and they set all their prisoners together and made them to promise how that, rescue or no rescue, they should be their prisoners. After that they made all their minstrels to blow up all at once and made the greatest revel of the world. Lightly it is the usage of Scots, that when they be thus assembled together in arms, the foot-men beareth about their neck horns in manner like hunters, some great, some small, of all sorts, so that when they blow all at once, they make such a noise, that it may be heard nigh four miles off: thus they do to abash their enemies and to rejoice themselves. When the bishop of Durham with his banner and ten thousand men with him were approached within a league, then the Scots blew their horns in such wise, that it seemed that all the devils in hell had been among them, so that such as heard them and knew not of their usage were sore abashed. This blowing and noise endured a long space and then ceased: and by that time the Englishmen were within less than a mile. Then the Scots began to blow again and made a great noise, and as long endured as it did before. Then the bishop approached with his battle well ranged in good order and came within the sight of the Scots, as within two bow-shot or less: then the Scots blew again their horns a long space. The bishop stood still to see what the Scots would do and aviewed them well and saw how they were in a strong ground greatly to their advantage. Then the bishop took counsel what was best for him to do; but all things well advised, they were not in purpose to enter in among the Scots to assail them, but returned without doing of anything, for they saw well they might rather lose than win.

When the Scots saw the Englishmen recule and that they should have no battle, they went to their lodgings and made merry, and then ordained to depart from thence. And because that sir Ralph Percy was sore hurt, he desired of his master that he might return to Newcastle or into some place, whereas it pleased him, unto such time as he were whole of his hurts, promising, as soon as he were able to ride, to return into Scotland, other to Edinboro or into any other place appointed. The earl of March, under whom he was taken, agreed thereto and delivered him a horse litter and sent him away; and by like covenant divers other knights and squires were suffered to return and took term other to return or else to pay their finance, such as they were appointed unto. It was shewed by me by the information of the Scots, such as had been at this said battle that was between Newcastle and Otterburn in the year of our Lord God a thousand three hundred four-score and eight, the nineteenth day of August, how that there were taken prisoners of the English party a thousand and forty men, one and other, and slain in the field and in the chase eighteen hundred and forty, and sore hurt more than a thousand: and of the Scots there were a hundred slain, and taken in the chase more than two hundred: for as the Englishmen fled, when they saw any advantage they returned again and fought: by that means the Scots were taken and none otherwise. Every man may well consider that it was a well fought field, when there were so many slain and taken on both parties.

After this battle thus finished, every man returned, and the earl Douglas' dead body chested and lain in a chare, and with him sir Robert Hart and Simon Glendowyn, then they prepared to depart: so they departed and led with them sir Henry Percy and more than forty knights of England, and took the way to the abbey of Melrose. At their departing they set fire in their lodgings, and rode all the day, and yet lay that night in the English ground: none denied them. The next day they dislodged early in the morning and so came that day to Melrose. It is an abbey of black monks on the border of both realms. There they rested and buried the earl James Douglas. The second day after his obsequy was done reverently, and on his body laid a tomb of stone and his banner hanging over him. Whether there were as then any more earls of Douglas, to whom the land returned, or not, I cannot tell; for I, sir John Froissart, author of this book, was in Scotland in the earl's castle of Dalkeith, living earl William, at which time he had two children, a son and a daughter; but after there were many of the Douglases, for I have seen a five brethren, all squires, bearing the name of Douglas, in the king of Scotland's house, David; they were sons to a knight in Scotland called sir James Douglas, and they bare in their arms gold, three oreilles gules, but as for the heritage, I know not who had it: as for sir Archambault Douglas, of whom I have spoken before in this history in divers places, who was a valiant knight and greatly redoubted of the Englishmen, he was but a bastard.

When these Scots had been at Melrose Abbey and done there all that they came thither for, then they departed each from other and went into their own countries, and such as had prisoners, some led them away with them and some were ransomed and suffered to return. Thus the Englishmen found the Scots right courteous and gentle in their deliverance and ransom, so that they were well content. This was shewed me in the country of Bearn in the earl of Foix's house by a knight named John of Chateauneuf, who was taken prisoner at the same journey under the banner of the earl of March and Dunbar: and he greatly praised the said earl, for he suffered him to pass in manner as he desired himself.

Thus these men of war of Scotland departed, and ransomed their prisoners as soon as they might right courteously, and so returned little and little into their own countries. And it was shewed me and I believe it well, that the Scots had by reason of that journey two hundred thousand franks for ransoming of prisoners: for with the battle that was before Stirling in Scotland, whereas sir Robert of Bruce, sir William Douglas, sir Robert Versy, sir Simon Fraser and other Scots chased the Englishmen three days, they never had journey so profitable nor so honourable for them, as this was. When tidings came to the other company of the Scots that were beside Carlisle, how their company had distressed the Englishmen beside Otterburn, they were greatly rejoiced, and displeased in their minds that they had not been there. Then they determined to dislodge and to draw into their own countries, seeing their other company were withdrawn. Thus they dislodged and entered into Scotland.

THE ANCIENT BALLAD OF CHEVY-CHASE

The First Fit (Fight)

The Persè out of Northombarlande,
    And a vowe to God mayd he,
That he wolde hunte in the mountayns
    Off Chyviat within dayes thre,
In the spite of doughtè Dogles,
    And all that ever with him be.
The fattiste hartes in all Cheviat
    He sayd he wold kill, and cary them away:
Be my feth, sayd the doughte Doglas agayn,
    I wyll hinder that hontyng yf that I may.

Then the Persè out of Banborowe* cam,
    With him a myghtye company;
With fifteen hondrith archares bold;
    The wear chosen out of shires thre.

This begane on a monday at morn
    In Cheviat the hillys so high;
The chyld may rue that ys un-born,
    It was the mor pitté.

The dryvars thorowe the woodes went
    For to rouse the dear;
Bowmen skirmished upon the rough grass
    With their browd arrows clear.
Then the wild deer thorowe the woodes went
    On every syde entirely;
Greyhounds through the bushes glent
    For to kyll thear deer.

The begane in Chyviat the hyls above
    Early on a monday;
Be that it drewe to the hour of noon
    A hondrith fat hartes ded ther lay.

The blew a mort† uppone the bent,
    They semblyd on all sides;
To the quarry then the Persé went
    To se the cutting up off the deare.

He sayd, It was the Duglas promys
    This day to meet me hear;
But I wyste he wold faylle truly:
    A gret oth the Persè swear.

At the laste a squyar of Northombelonde
    Looked at his hand full ny,
He was aware of the doughetie Doglas comynge:
    With him a mightè company,

*Bamburgh
†The name of the notes blown at the death of the stag.

Both with spear, battle-axe and brande*:
   Yt was a myghti sight to se.
Hardyar men both off hart nor hand
   Wear not in Christiantè.

The wear twenty hondrith spear-men good
   Withouten any fayle;
The wear borne a-long be the watter a Twyde,
   In the bowndes of Tividale.

Leave off the cutting up of the dear, he sayde,
   And to your bowys look ye tayk good heed;
For never since ye wear on your mothars borne
   Had ye never so mickle need.

The dougheti Dogglas on a stede
   He rode att his men beforne;
His armor glytteryde as dyd a red hot coal;
   A bolder barne was never borne.

Tell me 'what' men ye ar, he says,
   Or whos men that ye be:
Who gave youe leave to hunte in this
   Chyviat chase in the spyt of me?

The first man that ever him an answear mayd,
   Yt was the good lord Persè:
We wyll not tell the 'what' men we ar, he says,
   Nor whos men that we be;
But we wyll hount hear in this chase
   In the spyte of thyne, and of the.

The fattiste hartes in all Chyviat
   We have kyld, and cast to carry them a-way.
Be my troth, sayd the doughtè Dogglas agayn,
   Ther-for the one of us shall de this day.

*Sword

Then sayd the doughtè Doglas
   Unto the lord Persè:
To kyll all thes giltless men,
   A-las! it wear great pittè.

But, Persè, thowe art a lord of lande,
   I am an earl callyed within my contre;
Let all our men apart stande;
   And do the battell off the and of me.

Nowe Criste's curse on his crowne, sayd the lord
   Who-soever ther-to says nay,   [Persè,
Be my troth, doughtè Doglas, he says,
   Thow shall never se that day;

Nethar in Ynglonde, Scotland, nar France,
   Nor for no man of a woman born,
But and fortune be my chance,
   I dar met him on man for on.

Then bespayke a squyar off Northombarlonde,
   Rog. Widdrington was his nam;
It shall never be told in Sothe-Ynglonde, he says,
   To kyng Herry the fourth for sham.

I wat youe byn great lordes two,
   I am a poor squyar of lande;
I wyll never se my captayne fyght on a fylde,
   And stande my selffe, and looke on.
But whyll I may my weppone wield,
   I wyll not 'fayl' both harte and hande.

That day, that day, that dredfull day:
   The first FIT here I fynde.
And youe wyll here any mor athe hountyng athe
   Yet ys ther mor behynde.   [Chyviat,

The Second Fit

The Yngglishe men hade ther bowys yebent,
 Ther hartes were good yenoughe;
The first of arros that the shote off,
 Seven skore spear-men the slew.

Yet abides the yerle Doglas uppon the bent,
 A captayne good yenoughe,
And that was seen truly,
 For he wrought him both woo and mischief.

The Dogglas parted his host in thre,
 Lyk a cheffe cheften off pryde,
With sure speares off mighty tre
 The come in on every syde.

Thrughe our Ynglishe archery
 Gave many a wounde full wyde:
Many a doughty man they made to die
 Which gained them no pryde.

The Ynggllyshe men let thear bowys be,
 And pulde owt brandes that wer bright;
It was a hevy syght to se
 Bryght swordes on helmets lyght.

Thorowe ryche coat of mail, and many folds
 Many sterne the stroke downe streght:
Many a man, that was full free,
 Ther undar foot dyd lyght.

At last the Duglas and the Persè met,
 Lyk to captayns of myght and mayne;
The swapte together tyll the both swat
 With swordes, that wear of Milan.*

---

*Steel

Thes worthè persons for to fyght
    Ther-to the wear full fayne,
Tyll the bloode owte off thear helmets spurted,
    As ever dyd heal or rayne.*

Holde the, Persè, sayd the Doglas,
    And in faith I shall the bring
Wher thowe shalte have an earl's wages
    Of Jamy our Scottish kynge.

Thou shalte have thy ransom fre,
    I promise the here this thinge,
For the manfullyste man yet art thowe,
    That ever I conqueryd in field fightyng.

Nay 'then' sayd the lord Persè,
    I tolde it the beforne,
That I wolde never yielded be
    To no man of a woman born.

With that ther cam an arrowe hastely
    From off a mightie one,
Hit hathe stricken the earl Duglas
    In at the brest bane.

Thoroue lyvar and lungs bathe
    The sharp arrowe ys gane,
That never after in all his lyffe days
    He spake mo wordes but ane,
That was, Fyghte ye, my merry men, whyllys ye
    For my lyff days be gone.   [may,

The Persè leanyde on his brande,
    And sawe the Duglas de;
He tooke the dead man be the hande,
    And sayd, Wo ys me for the!

---

*Hail or rain

To have savyde thy lyffe I wold have pertyd with
   My landes for years thre,
For a better man of hart, nare of hande
   Was not in all the north countrè.

Of all that se a Skottishe knyght,
   Was called Sir Hewe the Mongon-byrry,
He sawe the Duglas to the death was dyght;
   He grasped a spear a trusti tre:

He rod uppon a steed
   Throughe a hundred archery;
He never stopped, nar never lingered,
   Tyll he cam to the good lord Persè.

He set uppone the lord Persè
   A blow, that was full soare:
With a sure spear of a myghtè tre
   Clean thorow the body he the Persè bore.

Athe tothar syde, that a man myght se,
   A large cloth yard and mare:
Towe bettar captayns wear nat in Christiantè,
   Then that day slain wear ther.

An archar off Northomberlonde
   Saw slean was the lord Persè,
He bar a bent bow in his hande,
   Was made off trusti tre:

An arow, that a cloth yarde was lang,
   To th'hard stele halyde he;
A blow, that was both sad and soar,
   He sat on Sir Hewe the Mongon-byrry.

The blow yt was both sad and sar,
   That he of Mongon-byrry sete;
The swan feathers that his arrowe bore,
   With his hart blood the wear wete.

Ther was never a freake wone foot wolde fle,
  But still in stour dyd stand,
Heawyng on yche othar, whyll the myght suffer,
  With many a bal-ful brande.

This battell begane in Chyviat
  An hour before the noon,
And when even-song bell was rang
  The battell was nat half done.

The tooke 'on' on ethar hand
  Be the lyght off the mone;
Many hade no strenght for to stande,
  In Chyviat the hyllys above.

Of fifteen hundred archars of Ynglonde
  Went away but fifti and thre;
Of twenty hundred spear-men of Skotlande,
  But even five and fifti:

But all wear slayne Cheviat within:
  The hade no strengthe to stand on hie;
The chylde may rue that ys un-borne,
  It was the mor pittè.

Thear was slayne with the lord Persè
  Sir John of Agerstone,
Sir Roge the gentle Hartly,
  Sir Wyllyam the bolde Hearone,

Sir Jorg the worthè Lovele,
  A knyght of great renowen,
Sir Raff the ryche Rugbè
  With blows wear beaten dowene.

For Wetharryngton my harte was wo,
  That ever he slayne shulde be;
For when both his leggis wear hewyne in to,
  Yet he knyled and fought on hys kne.

Ther was slayne with the dougheti Douglas
    Sir Hewe the Mongon-byrry,
Sir Davye Lwdale, that worthè was,
    His sistar's son was he:

Sir Charles a Murrè, in that place,
    That never a foot wolde fle;
Sir Hewe Maxwell, a lorde he was,
    With the Duglas dyd he dey.

So on the morrowe the mayde them byears
    Of byrch, and hasell so 'gray;'
Many widows with wepyng tears
    Cam to fetch their mates a-way.

Tivydale may complain thro' care,
    Northombarlond may mayk grat mone,
For towe such captayns, as slayne wear thear,
    On the march perti* shall never be none.

Word ys come to Edinburgh,
    To Jamy the Skottische kyng,
That dougheti Duglas, lyff-tenant of the Merches,
    He lay slean Chyviot with-in.

His handdes dyd he weal and wryng,
    He says, Alas, and woe ys me!
Such another captayn Skotland within,
    He says, y-feth shuld never be.

Worde ys come to lovly Londone
    Till the fourth Harry our kyng,
That lord Persè, leyff-tennante of the Merchis,
    He lay slayne Chyviat within.

---

*The parts lying upon the Marches

147

God have merci on his soll, sayd kyng Harry,
    Good lord, yf thy will it be!
I have a hundred captayns in Ynglonde, he sayd,
    As good as ever was hee:
But Persè, and I enjoy my lyffe,
    Thy deth well requited shall be.

As our noble kyng made his a-vowe,
    Lyke a noble prince of renowen,
For the deth of the lord Persè,
    He dyd the battel of Hombyll-down.

Wher syx and thirty Skottish knyghtes
    On a day wear beaten down:
Glendale glytteryde on ther armor bryght,
    Over castill, towar, and town.

This was the hontynge off the Cheviat;
    That tearing begane this spurn:
Old men that knowen the grownde well yenoughe,
    Call it the Battell of Otterborn.

At Otterburn began this spurne
    Uppon a Monday:
Ther was the doughtè Doglas slean,
    The Persè never went away.

Ther was never a tym on the march partes
    Sen the Doglas and the Persè met,
But yt was marvele, and the redde blude ronne not,
    As the rain does in the street.

Jhesue Christ remedy our evils,
    And to the blys us brynge!
Thus was the hountynge of the Chevyat:
    God send us all good ending.

Yt felle abowght the Lamasse tyde,
  When husbonds were getting in their hay,
The dowghtye Dowglasse prepared hym to ryde,
  In Ynglond to take a prey:

The yerlle of Fyffe, withowghten stryffe,
  He hied him over Solway:
The grete wolde ever together ryde;
  That race they may rue for aye.

Over 'Ottercap' hyll they came in,
  And so dowyn by Rodelyffecragge,
Upon Grene 'Leyton' the lyghted dowyn,
  Stirring many a stagge;

And boldely burnt Northomberlonde,
  And pillaged many a towyn;
They dyd owr Ynglyssh men great wrong,
  To battell that were not gone.

Then spake a man upon the bent,
  Of comforte that was not colde,
And sayd, We have burnt Northomberlond,
  We have all welth in holde.

Now we have haryed all Bamboroweshyre,
  All the welth in the worlde have wee;
I advise we ryde to Newe Castell,
  So styll and stoutly.

Uppon the morowe, when it was daye,
  The standards shone fulle bryght;
To the Newe Castelle they tooke the waye,
  And thether they cam fulle ryght.

Sir Henry Percy laye at the New Castelle,
  I telle yow withowten dread;
He had byn a March-man* all hys dayes,
  And kepte Barwyke upon Twede.

To the Newe Castell when they cam,
  The Skottes they cryde aloud,
Sir Harye Percy, and thow art within,
  Come to the fylde, and fyght:

For we have burnt Northomberlonde,
  Thy heritage good and ryght;
And since my lodging I have taken,
  With my brande dubbyd many a knyght.

Sir Harry Percy cam to the walles,
  The Skottyssh army to see;
'And thow hast burnt Northomberlond,
  Full sore it pains me.

Yf thou hast haryed all Bambarowe shyre,†
  Thow hast done me grete injury;
For the trespasse thow hast me done,
  The one of us schall dye.'

Where schall I byde the? sayd the Dowglas,
  Or where wylte thow come to me?
'At Otterborne in the hygh way,
  Ther maist thow well logeed be.

The roe full fearless there she runs,
  To make the game and glee:
The falcon and the pheasant both,
  Amonge the woodes on high.

---

*Borderer
†A large tract of land, which takes its name from the town and castle of Bamborough, formerly the residence of the Northumbrian kings.

Ther maist thow have thy welth at wyll,
   Well looged ther maist be.
Yt schall not be long, or I com the tyll,'
   Sayd Syr Harry Percye.

Ther schall I byde the, sayd the Dowglas,
   By the fayth of my bodye.
Thether schall I com, sayd Syr Harry Percy;
   My trowth I plyght to the.

A pype of wyne he gave them over the walles,
   For soth, as I yow saye:
Ther he mayd the Douglas drynke,
   And all hys hoste that daye.

The Dowglas turnyd him homewarde agayne,
   For soth withowghten naye,
He tooke his logeyng at Oterborne
   Uppon a Wedyns-day:

And ther he pitched hys standerd dowyn,
   Hys booty more and lesse,
And then he warned hys men to goo
   To chose ther geldyngs gresse.

A Skottyshe knyght hovered upon the bent,
   A spy I dare well says:
So was he aware on the noble Percy
   In the dawnynge of the daye.

He spurred to his pavyleon dore,
   As faste as hy myght ronne,
Awaken, Dowglas, cryed the knyght,
   For hys love, that sits in throne.

Awaken, Dowglas, cryed the knyght,
   For thow maiste waken wyth joy:
Yonder have I spyed the prowde Percy;
   And seven standerdes wyth hym.

Nay, by my trowth, the Douglas sayd,
　It ys but a false tale:
He durste not loke on my broad banner,
　For all Ynglonde so strong.

Was I not yesterdaye at the Newe Castell,
　That stonds so fayre on Tyne?
For all the men the Percy hade,
　He could not force me once to dine.

He stepped owt at hys pavelyon dore,
　To loke and it were lesse;
Araye yow, lordyngs, one and all,
　For here bygynnes no peysse.

The yerle of Menteith, thow arte my kinsman,
　The van I gyve to the;
The yerlle of Huntley cautious and keen,
　He schall wyth the be.

The lord of Buchan in armure bryght
　On the other hand he schall be;
Lorde Jhonstone, and lorde Maxwell,
　They to schall be with me.

Swinton fayre fylde upon your pryde
　To batell make yow ready:
Syr Davy Scotte, Syr Walter Stewart,
　Sir Jhon of Agurstone.

A Fytte

The Percye came before hys hoste,
　Wych was ever a gentyll knyght,
Upon the Dowglas lowde can he crye,
　I wyll holde that I have highte*

---

*Engaged

152

For thow haste burnt Northumberlonde
   And done me grete envye;
For thys trespasse thou haste me done,
   The one of us schall dye.

The Dowglas answerde hym agayne
   With grete wurds up on 'hee',
And sayd, I have twenty agaynst 'thy' one
   Byholde and thow maiste see.

Wyth that the Percye was grevyd sore,
   For sothe as I yow saye:
He lyghted dowyn upon his fote,
   And let go his horsse clene away.

Every man sawe that he dyd soo,
   That royal was ever in rout;
Every man let go hys horsse him froo,
   And lyght hym round about.

Thus Syr Hary Percye toke the fylde,
   For soth, as I yow saye:
Jesu Cryste in heaven on high
   Dyd helpe hym well that daye.

But nyne thowzand, ther was no moo;
   The cronykle will not layne*
Forty thowsande Skottes and fowre
   That day fowght them agayne.

But when the batell byganne to joyne,
   In hast ther cam a knyght,
'Then' letters fayre furth hath he tayne,
   And thus he sayd full ryght:

*Lie

153

My lorde, your father he gretes yow well,
  Wyth many a noble knyght;
He desyres yow to byde
  That he may see thys fyght.

The Baron of Grastoke ys com owt of the west,
  Wyth hym a noble companye;
All they loge at your father's thys nyght,
  And the Battel fayne wold they see.

For Jesu's love, sayd Syr Harye Percy,
  That dyed for yow and me,
Go to my lorde my Father agayne,
  And saye thow saw me not with yee:

My trowth ys plyght to yonne Skottysh knyght,
  It nedes me not to layne,
That I schulde byde hym upon thys bent,
  And I have hys trowth agayne:

And if that I wende off thys grownde
  For soth unfoughten awaye,
He wolde me call but a kowarde knyght
  In hys londe another daye.

Yet had I sooner be torn and rente,
  By Mary that mykel may*;
Than ever my manhood schulde be reprovyd
  With a Skotte another daye.

Wherfore schote, archars, for my sake,
  And let scharpe arowes flee:
Mynstrells, playe up for your reward,
  And well quyt it schall be.

---

*Maid

Every man thynke on hys trewe love,
    And marke hym to the Trenite:
For to God I make myne avowe
    Thys day wyll I not fle.

The blodye Harte in the Dowglas armes,
    Hys standerde stode on hye;
That every man myght full well knowe:
    By syde stode Starres thre:

The whyte Lyon on the Ynglysh parte,
    Forsoth as I you say;
The Lucetts and the Cressawnts both:
    The Skotts faught them agayne.

Uppon sent Andrewe lowde cane they crye,
    And thrysse they shout on hyght,
And syne marked them one owr Ynglysshe men,
    As I have tolde yow ryght.

Sent George the bryght owr ladye's knyght,
    To name they were full fayne,
Owr Ynglysshe men they cryde on hyght,
    And thrysse the schowtte agayne.

Wyth that scharpe arowes bygan to flee,
    I tell yow in certain;
Men of armes byganne to joyne;
    Many o dowghty man was ther slayne

The Percy and the Dowglas mette,
    That ether of other was fayne;
They struck together, whyll that the swette,
    With swords of fyne Cologne.

Tyll the bloode from ther helmets ranne,
    As the mist doth in the rayne.
Yelde the to me, sayd the Dowglas,
    Or ells thow schalt be slayne:

For I see, by thy bryght helmet,
    Thow arte sum man of myght:
And so I do by thy burnysshed brande,
    Thow art an yerle, or ells a knyght.

By my good faythe, sayd the noble Percy,
    Now haste thou rede full ryght,
Yet wyll I never yelde to the,
    Whyll I may stonde and fyght.

They struck together, whyll that they swette,
    Wyth swordes scharpe and long;
Ych on other so faste they beette,
    Tyll ther helmes cam in peyses dowyn.

The Percy was a man of strenghth,
    I tell yow in thys stounde,
He smote the Dowglas at the sworde's length,
    That he felle to the growynde.

The sworde was scharpe and sore can byte,
    I tell yow in sertayne;
To the harte he cowde hym smyte,
    Thus was the Dowglas slayne.

The stonderds stode styll on eke syde,
    With many a grevous grone;
Ther the fowght the day, and all the nyght,
    And many a dowghty man was 'slone'.

Ther was no man, that ther wolde flye,
    But styffly in stowre can stond,
Each one hewyng on other whyll they myght drye,
    Wyth many a bayllefull bronde.*

---

*Bayllefull bronde=hurtful sword

Ther was slayne upon the Skottes syde,
  For soth and sertenly,
Sir James a Dowglas ther was slayne,
  That daye that he cowde dye.

The Yerlle Mentaye of he was slayne,
  Dreadfully groaned uppon the growynd;
Sir Davy Scotte, Syr Walter Steward,
  Syr 'John' of Agurstone.

Syr Charlles Morrey in that place,
  That never a fote wold flye:
Sir Hughe Maxwell, a lorde he was,
  With the Dowglas dyd he dye.

Then was ther a Scottyshe prisoner tayne,
  Sir Hughe Mongomery was hys name,
For truth as I yow saye,
  He redeemed the Percy home agayne.

Now let us all for the Percy praye
  To Jesu most of myght,
To bryng hys sowle to the blysse of heven,
  For he was a gentyll knyght.

Index

(Roman numerals in italic refer to the maps)

158

159